I0035798

YOUR WAKE-UP CALL

Your Guide to Motivation, Inspiration & Enthusiasm

YOUR WAKE-UP CALL

Your Guide to Motivation, Inspiration & Enthusiasm

Charles D.A. Ruffolo – MPA, The NetworKing
Bestseller author of Network Your Way To Success

Foreword by Stedman Graham

Edited by Anne Marie Westra-Nijhuis

Colofon

Copyright ©2014	Charles D.A. Ruffolo – The NetworKing BV
Publisher	The NetworKing / Leonon Media
Author	Charles D.A. Ruffolo – The NetworKing BV
Editor	Anne Marie Westra-Nijhuis – EPLÚ Management Support
Proofreaders	Ashley Corbett and Joyce Garritano
Cover Design	The NetworKing BV
Inside Design	Leonon Media
Photographs	Maik Hewitt (www.masaypics.com)
ISBN:	978-94-91480-096

All rights reserved. No part of this publication may be reproduced or transmitted in any form or by any means, electronic of mechanical, including photocopying, recording, or by any information storage and retrieval system, without permission in writing from the Author – Charles D.A. Ruffolo.

TESTIMONIALS

"Charles walked into my business class with an amazing amount of confidence for a sophomore in high school. I knew immediately that he would add the spark, sense of humor, and talent that every teacher hopes for in a student. He definitely did not disappoint me! I espcially enjoyed watching him interact with all of the class and even when he was making us laugh, I could see the respect he established with his classmates. I am so very proud to see all that he has accomplished and has still remained sincere and humble."

Joyce Garritano - Business Education Teacher Norwin Senior High School

"I remember, walking with my best friend, and talking about the title for his new book It was for sure, the book should be about taking your own responsibility, values and norms in life and about giving back to your network. Giving back to other people you do not know yet, and giving others a hand when they need it. Ruf is a great example of someone who is not waiting for things to happen in life, but taking his own responsibility to make things happen. So when life seems hard and difficult... Take your responsibility, get into action, show love and respect, as This is YOUR "Wake-Up Call"!

Martijn de Looze - Area Manager ICI PARIS XL Netherlands at A.S. Watson Luxury, Perfumeries & Cosmetics

"Charles Ruffolo is a man with a unique outlook on the business world based on a lifetime of both success and failure. He illustrates the tough decisions that are needed to "win the battle we call life."

General Wesley K. Clark (ret) – *Former NATO's Supreme Allied Commander, Europe & CEO of Wesley K. Clark & Associates.*

"Your Wake-Up Call" is an inspiring book by an inspiring person. Since the day I met Ruf my life changed. His vision, his passion and commitment to live and people is a true inspiration. Never give up when you're challenged and never lose faith. And above all never lose faith in yourself. Thank you Ruf for being my *"Wake-Up Call"* all these years."

Fatima Elatik - *District Mayor of Amsterdam East & Ambassador of Giving Back Foundation*

"What a privilege to experience up close the overwhelmingly inspirational life of my dear friend Charles Ruffolo, now available for everyone with this book. His gift is bringing a little bit of heaven into people's lives, which is truly supernatural while keeping' it real whether times are good or bad."

Patrick America - *Diamond Trader & Social Investor*

DEDICATION

This book is dedicated to my wife, Herma, first and foremost, and to Joe P., Clara E., Papa, Mama, Tony, Mary, Joe, Gerry, Jackie, Bobby, Jeannie, Hawk, Mike, Fern, Barbara, Kathy, Maureen, Angela, Eke, Reina, Wendy, Louise, Anneke, Anne Marie, Ashley, Mrs G., the entire The NetworKing Network and to God.

Charles D.A. Ruffolo - MPA
Professional Networker, International Speaker,
Trainer, Moderator & Author

The *Networ***King** ®

TABLE OF CONTENTS

FOREWORD

Charles "Ruf" Ruffolo displays a strong sense of purpose and personal commitment to accelerate the positive attitudes of others within his network. As you read his book, "*Your Wake-Up Call*," you will learn how he came to chose ten of what he thinks are the most powerful characteristics one can possess. Those that illustrate inner strength to be self- inspired, self-motivated and enthused in life.

Charles wants us all to know, that the building blocks for LIFE are within each of us. They enable us to reach success, even when faced with the probability of failure. Empowering those around him, Charles has the ability to identify and inspire the inner strength of others to help them endure and overcome any situation. He invites them to reach high, not by longing for the things they do not possess, but by appreciating that which they do.

This commitment is also illustrated by his need to give back to others in his network. He is committed to helping others and has done so for many years through an organization that he established called, the Giving Back Foundation. It is a Foundation that I am pleased to be a part of, and one that offers an annual Scholarship in my name to one of the most prestigious Universities in the Netherlands. I was also moved when Charles energized his network to have a United States Flag flown over the US Capital in my name. It was a token of appreciation for my work with self-identity and education, and I am thankful.

This book reveals the true story of a man who tells it like it really is, has love in his heart and a genuine concern for others in his network. It is my honor to introduce and contribute something for my friend, and one whose many friends know him as The NetworKing!

Stedman Graham
CEO of S. Graham & Associates

A TRIBUTE TO CHARLES

Charles, you are a purely giver. Rarely have I seen someone as generous as you are, someone who sees it as his duty to give. "I just have to give, do something for someone else, that gives me a good feeling inside and it makes me happy," you always say. Undoubtedly you put aside any self-interest; you give just to give which makes you who you are, a beautiful person!

I am very proud that, because of you, I am part of the invaluable support of your Giving Back Foundation for some years now. With this Foundation you offer ambitious school and college students equal opportunities in order to become successful, whatever their background may be.

Dear Charles, it is my honor and I am privileged to know you, to work with you, to maintain a close friendship with you and, last but not least, to keep you out of trouble!

Your only business partner and very dear friend,

Anne Marie Westra-Nijhuis

Professional in project & event management, communications & marketing
EPLÚ Management Support, the Netherlands
www.e-plu.nl - annemariewestra@e-plu.nl

INTRODUCTION

How did I come up with the title for this book? I always say: "Everyone is born with a network, and through life, your network grows, based on your values and norms and the respect that you earn through your actions to give back. With this book, I wanted to "Wake You Up" to what you already have, and provide you a guide to inspire, motivate and enthuse yourself and others to be successful in networking.

After thinking about what woke me up to networking, and looking back on what networking is all about and where my network comes from, I remembered the song, "***Born to Be Wild***," written by Mars Bonfire and performed by Steppenwolf:

"*Get your motor runnin'*
Head out on the highway
Looking for adventure
In whatever comes our way

Yeah, darlin'
Gonna make it happen
Take the world in a love embrace
Fire all of your guns at once
And explode into space

I like smoke and lightnin'
Heavy metal thunder
Racing in the wind
And the feeling that I'm under

Like a true nature child
We were born
Born to be wild

We can climbed so high
I never wanna die
Born to be wild
Born to be wild"

I think the lyrics clearly explain and point out what networking is all about.

The song starts out very clearly: *"Get your motor runnin,"* which means that you have to get your act together (*Your Wake-Up Call*) and from the starting block of life you need to prepare yourself for networking, based on our values and norms system (Chapter 1). The song goes on to say: *"We were born, Born to be wild, We can climbed so high,"* meaning that we were *"Born to Network"* and want to climb so high to be successful in our lives. Success is built on the character you possess and your behavior toward others in your network (Chapter 2). We all are *"Looking for adventure."* No-one just wants to sit back and watch things happening in their network, or faith and hope to make things happen (Chapter 3). *"Head out on the highway"*; your life, your networking story is an adventure; it's a journey on the highway of life and it is your route to success – now tell the trust and earn the respect from others in your network (Chapter 4). But first you have to wake up to the sounds of the triumphs and buglers that were used when you were born, and use the elements of life that you will learn and are addressed in my book, *"Your Wake-Up Call."*

But there will be curves, bends, turns, valleys and hills to climb in our lives, as the song goes on to say, *"Whatever comes our way."* So are you ready to *"Head out on the highway"* in search of adventure? Will you give up your integrity and empathy for others in your network (Chapter 5)?

We may think that others have a smoother ride on that networking highway of life, but *"Yeah, darling,"* you are *"gonna make it happen,"* and no one else is going to display the strong character, conviction and perseverance that you need to be able to *"Take the world in a love embrace"* with your enthusiasm (Chapter 6). You will need to dig deep and be confronted with all the ills of our world and *"Fire all of your guns at once,"* meaning you need to adhere to your core value system and kick in your faith, hope, trust, respect, integrity, empathy, perseverance, enthusiasm, giving and love during your successes and failures in your life,; *"And explore into space"* (Chapter 7). Your steady unwavering character and behavior will be *"like smoke and lightnin', Heavy metal thunder, Racing in the wind, And the feeling that I'm under;"* putting you in control of your network by your networking actions in the modern world, using the social media platforms (Chapter 8). You will be either successful or unsuccessful, but your network knows who you are, *"Like a true nature child,"* a person that will climb so high and never wanna die, because you were "Born with Love to Give Back!" (Chapter 9.)

Why a book about Inspiration, Motivation and Enthusiasm?

Through the many years of training, lecturing, speaking and hosting networking events throughout the world, I have seen, heard and experienced that many people have the wrong perception of the power of networking. People often ask me how I got to be so inspired, motivated, enthused and maintain such a positive attitude. And I tell them that I keep the spirit and faith in networking alive in my heart and soul. I want to bring across this fact and to empower everyone that we were all born with a powerful network, but we don't think we have a network, or know how to energize it to reach the level of success we are pursuing at a certain moment in our lives. We think that networking is for wealthy people, the famous persons or the individuals that give us an impression that they have everything under control and things are going so well for them. As we look at others around us, we sometimes wonder how they keep inspired, motivated or even enthused at work, on the job, at home or in whatever situation they are forced in. Well I am here to tell you that the ingredients for this state of mind is within you, you just have to give it a *"Wake-up Call"*!

We often allow others to influence our mood and state of mind, our values and norms system, our character and type of behavior, our faith and hope beliefs, our ability to trust and respect others, our integrity and empathy for others, our perseverance and enthusiasm toward reaching our goals our determination and attitude to what is success or failure, and even how, what and when we need to give back the love to others in our network. I'm a firm believer that networking is a way of life, your life and we have to protect ourselves continuously from not giving up or abandoning our core value system. We have a built in value system and we need to learn how to unlock a very powerful force within ourselves by just turning the key, our personal key of life that will unleash in our mind the powerful ability to maintain inspiration, motivation and enthusiasm day-to-day under all networking circumstances or predicaments!

Networking is not what you want, but what others in your network need or want at that moment in their lives – please don't make the mistake that you think you have the best thing going. When we understand what networking is, we will quickly realize that we all are faced with the same challenges and obstructions.

So what is networking?

In my first book, "*Network Your Way To Success,*" I fully described what networking is. In short, Webster says that networking is "making connections among people or groups of a like kind." I say that networking is being able to help or benefit from contacts with individuals with whom you have a direct or indirect relationship; in short, a positive process of mutual support. It's about linking common interests that surface throughout life, about making connections among people you meet on a daily basis. It's about gathering and exchanging information, assistance, ideas, resources and advice. It's about benefiting from those vital links, and giving back in return.

Networking is no rocket science. It's a common sense way of life. But you have to learn the ropes, or the loop of success won't swing your way.

Networking is, indeed, a behavioral and organizational skill, but those are just fancy terms for something so basic and commonplace, that you already do it without thinking. Problem is that you most likely do it on such a minimal basis, that you may not recognize it, and, therefore, it barely impacts your life the way it could.

Networking is a philosophy of life. It's about not settling for the status quo.

It's a philosophy built on faith, hope, trust, respect, integrity, empathy, perseverance and making things happen with a lot of enthusiasm, even if you are successful or you fail to reach your goals. It is your ability to give back to others and love what you do in your network. It's an art of interacting with and influencing people while listening to their needs and wishes. And it's a science of chemistry between people in all walks of life. It's pure and practical and, above all, it works.

Contrary to popular opinion, networking is a lot more than marketing or selling. It's literally a way of life. Personally, networking helps me to deal with some of life's minor annoyances as well as my most challenging obstacles and opportunities. It helps me to identify clients and increase my profitability. It means exposure for me – as it will for you – in untold ways. You can learn how to foster and build a network from the ground up, and then make it a ritual in your daily life, the same as I've done with mine. When you do, you'll experience unfathomable rewards. Once you make it a habit, you'll wonder how you ever lived without consciously networking all the time. It's addictive – hopefully the best – or better yet the *only* – addiction you'll ever have.

I remember President Clinton reading from his book, "*My Life*," during an event I hosted for him in Amsterdam:

"I learned a lot from the stories my uncle, aunts, and grandparents told me: that no one is perfect but most people are good; that people can't be judged only by their worst or weakest moments; that harsh judgments can make hypocrites of us all; that a lot of life is just showing up and hanging on; that laughter is often the best, and sometimes the only, response to pain.
Perhaps most important, I learned that everyone has a story – of dreams and nightmares, hope and heartache, love and loss, courage and fear, sacrifice and selfishness."

Networking is based on a value system that was given to you, combined with the values of others, enabling you to develop your own set of values system for networking.

A set of values and norms that has others outside your network wanting to be a part of your network, wanting to be associated with you and your network, or wanting you to be a part of their network. We all want to be part of someone else's networking story and someone else wants to be part of your networking story, the journey, and our journey to successful networking. In your journey of life, you are building a memory, and those memories become your story that touches the lives and the hearts of others, sometimes without you even knowing!

Journey with me on the path of networking, discover that you were "Born to Network," and hear the trumpets and buglers playing **"Your Wake-Up Call!"**

As **Ralph Waldo Emerson** said:
"Make your own Bible. Select and collect all the words and sentences that in all your readings have been to you like the blast of a trumpet."

CHAPTER 1

VALUES & NORMS

"Your beliefs become your thoughts,
Your thoughts become your words,
Your words become your actions,
Your actions become your habits,
Your habits become your values,
Your values become your destiny."
Mahatma Gandhi

VALUES

A value is the regard that something is held to deserve; the importance or preciousness of something.

The best "value & norm system" is one where you don't have to look over your shoulder. Values do not demonstrate what you do, but express something about why you do things and why you will or will not undertake them.

What do you value the most in your life right now? Stop and think. What are the things you value the most? Did you always value them as you do right now? We all have our own values, and through our lives values are given, values will change, values are forgotten, and values identify who you are in life and in your network. Just like you, I have a value system that was given, learned, adapted, modified, adjusted, and accepted by myself and the people in my network.

Most of us learned our values or morals, if you prefer, at home, spiritual establishments, school, as members of organizations, or from the streets. Where do today's children or youth learn their values? Most likely they learn them from their parents, teachers and spiritual leaders, but also from a society that is constantly changing. Too often, today's youngsters are influenced by what they see and hear on television, the Internet, or on the streets. Even on social media platforms. Sometimes these social media platforms want us to believe everything we read, see, or hear without even investigating the source or finding out the truth of the information.

I learned a value system from my parents. They laid a foundation for me based on faith and from there I was exposed to a value system from the outside world; our society. A world, that doesn't always carry or honor some of the values I was taught, neither always wants to accept my value system. After being taught a value system and learning to accept a different one from others out of my network, I selected, combined, and adapted the values that fit best into my life and created my own value system. A value system that fit to my likings and one that complimented me; a value and norm system only for me, Charles Douglas Armando Ruffolo!

As I mentioned before, faith that was taught and given to me by my parents and family has been the primary source of my value system. I was instilled the foundation of faith in God, a loving and caring relationship with others, and a giving back principle for others in my network. I think a positive spiritual passion is the power source that transforms people into beautiful human beings whom are unselfish, generous, caring, loving, and compassionate. Please choose your values carefully. Pursue a positive faith that will boost and bless your values to shape you into a beautiful human being. Believe me, if you have a foundation that is based on a strong value system, your network will be there for you at all times and also be willing to work for and with you.

Let's emphasize certain things about values:
-    Values are more than a system of rules. They are a person's core ap-

proach to life.
- People have their own set of values.
- People are shaped by values.
- Values remind you to value people. Treat people with dignity and respect and don't violate the values of others. Respect their differences.
- Incorporate values into your own actions.
- Teach others to accept and live by values.

I have discovered and continue to learn that life is built on a strong value and norm system that forms the blocks of our networking L.I.F.E. I have narrowed them down to four building blocks that are stacked on top of each other, starting with Love as the basic building block.

L – LOVE = Love is an intense feeling of deep affection for someone or something. Love is the greatest gift given and is something that our parents continue to give us. From the moment we were born, our parents loved us. They gave us their unconditional love and shared their love for us with others in their network. Our foundation of love was laid, because we felt and learned what love is all about.

I – INTEGRITY = Integrity is doing what is right; legally and morally. It is steadfast adherence to a strict moral or ethical code. Our parents quickly taught us to be honest and not to lie to ourselves, them, or to others. Do you remember how your parents taught you to do things correctly? Taught you to adhere to the rules and the value system in your surrounding area, and to have a sound moral character? To do the right thing whether anyone was looking or not, not to cheat or to steal? Do you remember how your parents taught you to say *"please"* and *"thank you?"*

F – FAITH = Faith is a belief with strong conviction. It's a firm belief in something for which there may be no tangible proof. It's complete trust in or devotion to. Faith is the opposite of doubt. When we were at a very young age, for most of us, our parents already started teaching and sharing their faith with us. We saw our parents expressing or serving their faith. We saw a strong conviction towards something in their lives.

E – ENTHUSIASM = Enthusiasm is having a great excitement for or interest in a subject or cause. It's an intense and eager enjoyment, interest, or approval. It's an ecstasy power arising within us. At an early age, we started realizing that enthusiasm was being used to attract others to our network. We learned that no one can make you enthusiastic, because enthusiasm doesn't come from outside things; it comes from within you.

Values make up our character and show who we are and what we stand for. I think our value system is broken down into four stages in our lives. Values are built on the four foundation blocks of L.I.F.E. We have a foundation which was given to us in a value system that was passed down from our parents and most likely is the basic of our L.I.F.E. today – Love, Integrity, Faith and Enthusiasm.

I call my value system, which was established, fueled, and fed to me by my parents, family members, and friends around me Stage 1, the beginning stage of my learned behavior or programming stage.

The four stages of our value system, our outlook towards life are:

Stage 1 – Feed Value System: we are born, then given, taught, and fed a value system by our parents – this is from birth to about 9 years old.

Stage 2 – Exposed Value System: we experience firsthand the value system of the outside world; our society – this is from 10 till 18 years old.

Stage 3 – Own Value System: our own identity; a combination of the feed value system and the exposed value system – this is from 19 till about 25 years old.

Stage 4 – Adjustment Value System: the adjustments to our values are realized by a continuous development in and integration of values from others in our network or to the times at hand – this is from 26 onward for the rest of our life perhaps even into eternity.

The only hope of communication with our value system between networks is started by recognizing the radical difference in the values affirmed by others in our network. Our own personal value system is created by the values fed to us by our parents, together with what we are exposed to by the world, or society. A value system that in times will be adjusted or modified based on further developments or circumstances that face us in life. A value system we hope to continue to follow, but that could be much different than the one our parents fed us with. In our personal value system, we may be more interested in the value of pleasure as an end in itself than of giving to our network.

During the Feed Value System (0-9 years old), we choose not to do wrong or go off the value system that was taught to us by our parents or by our immediate network. We do this because of the fear of punishment or rejection. Once we are exposed to the value system of the world, we develop more experience and knowledge. We start to reason things through. If you were born into a family that practiced a particular value system, you are psychologically programmed by that cultural belief system. There are very few individuals who can honestly separate themselves from their formative psychological conditioning. In this stage of life, our parents are protecting us from the ills of society and exposing us to the truth of why things happen. We are protected from the truth of other people's actions. We didn't get the "*Wake-Up Call*" yet!

In the Exposed Value System (10-18 years old), we start making more educated decisions because we develop a sense of what we distinguish to be right from wrong in our own eyes. As we begin to interact more with networks outside our society, we gain more responsibilities and start understanding that rules and laws are created for the greater good of society. We begin to see our role in the big networking world growing. We start to understand and conclude what is right or wrong. The fear of the consequences of our actions is now taken into consideration, and we way the pros and cons of them. At this stage of networking, we begin to mature. At this stage of life, we begin to hear the trumpets from a distance, but cannot clearly hear our *"Wake-Up Call"* yet. We hear the sounds, but cannot or don't want to think they are meant for us.

In the next stage, we start creating our Own Value System (19 to 25 years old) by combining the values that our parents fed us with what society is exposing us to. We start creating our own value system. At this stage of networking, our lives will change as we get more experience and we grow older while being exposed to much more in life. This stage of our life deals with our interpersonal values and our will to complete our sense of personal identity. Who am I? What am I worth? What can I do that is important? In this stage of life we do hear the trumpets and buglers that give us the *"Wake-Up Call."* We now understand that they are playing for us and directing us to either get back on the right track or drift off further down the wrong path of life.

As we approach the Adjustment Value System (26 on to the rest of your life) within our life, we learn new untried ways of relating to others in our network. We relate to them to get our basic needs of love, acceptance, understanding, freedom, and achievement satisfied. We develop our own values and social culture from the environment we are raised in and continue to modify or adjust our value system to fit into the current circumstances or time we are living. From there we continue to form our own value system that engulfs the total process of networking in our lives. We hear the *"Wake-Up Call"* so well that we are blowing our own trumpet to others in our network.

Just remember that the set of values with which we are nurtured will govern the choices we make in life.

The effectiveness of networking values strings together as a necklace of trust that can only be accomplished when bound by the central strand. Each value may be valuable in itself, but only true trust of networking comes when held together by the binding power of giving back and love for yourself and others in your network.

It's amazing that if we all look back to what we have in common, we quickly recognize that when we were born we all were given a network from our parents. A powerful network – a network based on the principle that networking is a birthright, your birthright, and your right to succeed. Let's look back on it.

Stage 1: Feed Value System (ages 0-9 years)

We are born, given, taught, and fed a value system by our parents. A value system that we will protect at all costs. The values our parents taught us include faith, hope, and love. As we grow older and enter different stages of our lives, more values are added. Values are forgotten or placed aside, so we can better understand the meaning of networking.

Then we face our first confrontation with the values that our parents embedded into us. This confrontation could be at the school yard or on the sports field. Someone just doesn't like the way you look, the way you act, or the way you express yourself. You wonder to yourself: "What am I doing wrong, what did I say, or what did I wear to cause this confrontation? When I left home, everything was fine. When I walked down the street, everything was fine. But when I turned the corner and walked into the school yard or sports field, everything was different." In my case, JoAnn and her friends, her network, started laughing and joking about the way I was walking, talking, and dressing. For the first time, I had an odd feeling. There's someone in my network now making me feel bad or making fun of me. It was the first confrontation with somebody that had other values and norms then what I was fed. A confrontation I would have more than once.

At such a moment you start analyzing yourself and thinking what you have to change to be liked, not to be laughed at, and to be accepted. To be accepted into other people's network, because everybody wants to be accepted, everyone wants to be liked, and everyone wants to be loved. It's just a normal way of thinking; a normal way of life. That's when you bend and stray off the values and norms that your parents taught you. I didn't until I woke up, smelled the coffee, and had my "*Wake-Up Call.*" I realized that networking is not being accepted; networking is being you. It's based on your values and norms; a value system that grew from faith to hope, trust to respect, integrity to empathy, perseverance to enthusiasm, success to failure, and giving back to love. Your value system will influence the attitude and behavior of others in your network. Don't ever forget that!

When I was young (Stage 1), my mom (late Clara Elizabeth – Clara E.) used to take me with her to visit other family members and friends. I remember I always enjoyed those visits because I knew I was given so much love from my mother and her network. I was protected, cared for, and made to feel special. There was lots of food of course; excellent foods from Italian, Polish, Irish, Hungarian, and Soul food cultures. I could eat as much as I wanted. Not knowing at the time, my mother was trying to instill in me a solid value system. Some might say she was brainwashing me, but it was a wash job I needed. I remember once my mother asked me to tell all the people in the room what I was not going to do when I got older. It started out like this: *I was not going to drink, because that would turn me into an alcoholic. I was not going to take drugs, because that would turn me into a drug addict. I was not going to steal, because I would become a thief and end up in jail.* At later stages of life, I found out that these three things helped me to reach the false hope of success. I didn't keep those promises to myself, my mother, or to my network. I drank, took drugs, and I stole. I did go to jail (only for one night), and I did not pass GO several times like when you play the game of Monopoly!

As children, we are pretty simple. We usually wear our feelings on our sleeve; right out there in the open air for others in our network to see. We can say the most profound things in the most common ways. We have not been around the block or street long enough to become cynical or hardened by the world. We accept things, adapt, listen, conform, and we love naturally. I listened to my mother and grew into being The NetworKing, so I don't think the benefits of listening to her at a young age was so bad at all!

Stage 2: Exposed Value System (ages 10-18 years)
Our experience firsthand with the value system of the outside world; the society outside our own world.

The question during this period of your life is: will you let the value system you were fed fit into other people's network? Believe me, at first, you will until you feel the burning desire; the need to fall back on your own value system. I remember thinking that everyone else would have the value system that I was given – a value system based on family, faith, hope, and love.

From birth, we learn to crawl, to walk, and then to stand on our own two feet carrying with us the values that were fed to us. We thought only to be confronted with the rucksack of values that others had. Will you take something from other people's values, from their rucksack, and put them in your duffel bag? With the scrapes on your knees from crawling, you will be confronted with the value system of others, and you will add values to your system that you were never exposed to before. From there, your personal value system has been enlarged by the cultural and social value system of others who entered your network.

For example, you have a strong religious conviction and you fall in love with a person that has the same ambition and hope as you have. You find out that this person doesn't have a religion, so you are confronted with your basic personal values. What are you going to do? How far do you want to go to prevent your value system from clashing with the value system of another person; a person in this case that you love very much? You could choose to say: "I'm going to break this relationship because he or she doesn't have a religion." You could say:"I'll go my way and you go your way." You could say: "I'll try to instill my religion in him or her just as I have," or you could say: "You stay the way you are and I stay the way I am," because we love each other too much to break up.

Based on that strong love for each other, you eventually may compromise that your future children will be raised in to believe. It could become a conflict. Value systems will clash in networking, and how you handle that is based on your total value system. Values can become very confusing and fragmented during the stages of your value system. It often is not the abolishment of values but simply the replacement of one set of values with another.

This is just a small example of life. We are from different races, creeds, faiths and colors. Daily, we are confronted with the clash of different value systems. Whose choice do you think it is it to enlarge this value system? Of course, it's yours! You will base that new value system on what is best for you, on your exposure, and experience with other networks.

When I was growing up, I had a good friend, Peedy Cud, who was an African-American. Peedy's family moved up from the South (Alabama) to the North (Pittsburgh) and we became very good childhood friends. We had just entered the second stage of our value system. One day, Peedy would come over to our house to play and eat with me. Suddenly, out of the blue, Peedy asked my mother: "*Miss Clara, if I use Ivory Soap* (a white bar of soap), *can I wash myself white?*" My mom looked at him with an expression of sheer surprise on her face but with true love in her heart she answered: *"Peedy, what's wrong with you boy, you are just fine the way you are and don't you ever forget that! Now eat your sandwich and go outside and play."* At that time, I didn't understand what Peedy was really saying or why he was saying that until later when I moved onto the next stage in life. I saw first-hand that others did not have friends like I had; friends from all walks of life and society. I quickly got the *"Wake-Up Call"* when I joined the US Military at the age of 18 and met people who never saw an African-American or even snow fall from the sky before.

Stage 3: Creating Your Own Value System (ages 19 to 25 years)
The combination of the Feed Value System and the Exposed Value System creates our own identity; our Own Value System.

Did you ever hear a parent say: "Boy, I didn't raise you to be like that?" When parents say this, they mean their son or daughter's value system changed so much that it is not compatible anymore to how they raised their child.

This phase could be a painful but also an enriching phase of your life. It could be painful because you see the world in a different light now, and you could suffer from the conflict of values in your network. Please remember that life without suffering isn't life at all. We need to prepare ourselves for painful experiences like suffering, hardship, and being hurt. Suffering, hardship, and hurt will be coming. But also are happiness, joy, and love. So in order to become a person who is happy in all things, you must first become a person who can get through the trials and tribulations of life.
This way you will be able to enter the next stages of your life.

Some people live in a world of hate, greed, and envies; a world that doesn't love. You need to live in and see a world of acceptance, of empathy, and of love. During Stage 3, your value system will be tested. Will you compromise your value system? Will you give in? Will you bend? Or will you stand fast and not sway or bend to the likes of others? Only you can decide.

You yourself have to weigh the pros and cons. Do realize, however, that this can change your life. Be very careful in accepting the values of others.

In this stage of life, you are creating and combining your feed value system. The feed value system is a combination of the things you were exposed to and you experienced in your life and those of others in your network. Keep listening to "*Your Wake-Up Call*"! You will keep or trash some of the values. Remember, actions speak louder than words, so others will follow your actions in your network. Do you ever think about if something is right or wrong or if your decision is the correct one or not? Just listen to yourself. Listen to that feeling inside of you, your gut feeling. If you are having ill feelings about accepting or following the values of someone else in your network, then I would really question those values. As we all grow older, we continue to adjust our value system to fit the circumstances or the current time of our lives. We must realize that our society has a consensus on the extent to which diversity and different values are to be valued. Daily, we are bombarded with the values of not only ourselves but also of the world at large.

Stage 4: The Adjustments to Our Value System (ages 26 on to the rest of your life)

Our adjustments to our value system have been realized and our value system is in continuous development integrating the values of other people in our network or to the times at hand.

Adding and adjusting our value system with the values of others is a lifelong journey. This journey will take you to far off places and enlighten your life. You will be confronted with your basic values that your parents instilled in you. Take for example the love of your life we talked about before who doesn't have a religion. You go on vacation together to that far off place; that far off land that you both always wanted to go to. You arrive and see the beauty, but you also see the poverty in this country. At the same time, you look at your life and you see how enriched your life actually is.

You have enough food, running water, a nice house, two cars, paying job, life insurance, Internet on your phone, social media platforms, etc. These people are without electricity, and only have a candle to light their mud built house. You even brought a water bottle that has your company logo on it, because you wanted to promote your business. At the same time, these poor people don't have clean drinking water. Your heart is crying out; wanting to do something to help the people who live there in poverty. You start feeling empathy and you want to give back. Then, you suddenly find out that the love of your life doesn't have as much empathy for others as you do. You come to the conclusion that your value systems on this situation are not similar. What do you do? Are you going to work on adapting, changing, or influencing your partner's value system, or will you just accept your partner's value system and walk away from the empathy and love for others? In this stage of your value system, this is something that you will be faced with. Will you be able to blow your horn so loud that your partner hears the *"Wake-Up Call"* to the value of empathy and love? These additions or deletions of your value system will indicate if someone allows you into their network, or if they allow you to stay in your network. As I always say: "Everyone is born with a network and through life it grows based on his or her values."

NORMS

A norm is - something that is usual, typical, or standard or pattern - norms are the behavioral expectations and cues within a society or group.

Many would have us believe that networking is measured by our financial success and that we live in a world in which everything is material. Believe

31

in a world where power matters most; a dog eat dog world where you ought to look down on people. Believe in a world where lying is the right thing to do in a time of need, and anger is somehow a good thing.

I say that networking is based on a value and norm system that has us holding firm to and living in a world and a network that has a code of ethics. This code of ethics combines your qualities distinguishing you from others while having you react positively in response to the actions of others in your network. It has you maintaining a strong conviction while cherishing your desired outcome that enables you to have confidence while showing consideration for others in your network. It has you adhering to strong moral principles while being able to understand and share the feelings of others in your network, and has you holding on, despite difficulty or delay while digging deep for the power to achieve or reach your success. This code of ethics has you applying the cardinal rule of networking while displaying an intense feeling of deep affection to help others in your network. If you can understand and receive the knowledge of these elements of networking, everything will change in your life. That is something that I truly hope this book, "*Your Wake-Up Call*," will provide to you and your network! Our attitudes about the worth of people make up our values and norms system, therefore, our character and behavior toward others in our network. Chapter 1 kick started the importance of having values and norms in networking. It is highlighted and expressed in the first two lines of the song "*Get your motor runnin' Head out on the highway.*" From the starting block of life, we need to prepare ourselves for networking based on our values and norms. Get your act together and continue following me on the networking highway of life, "*Your Wake-Up Call*" to your success!

"If we aren't willing to pay a price for our values, if we aren't willing to make some sacrifices in order to realize them, then we should ask ourselves whether we truly believe in them at all."
Barack Obama

CHAPTER 2

CHARACTER & BEHAVIOR

"A good character is the best tombstone. Those who loved you and were helped by you will remember you when forget-me-nots have withered. Carve your name on hearts, not on marble."
Charles Spurgeon

CHARACTER

Character is defined as the combination of qualities, features, or attributes that distinguishes one person, group, or thing from another.

Realize that the people in your network, just like you, also come with character formed by their backgrounds, experiences, education, religion, and philosophical beliefs, and ultimately their own set of values and complex lifelong conglomeration.
The stepping stones of the values and norms in my life are the qualities, characteristics, and behavior I rely on to take me safely through all the challenges of my life and into my network. People (outside our network) who may want to be in our networks will look at our character traits and behavior to see if they really want to follow us or be part of our network.

Throughout many years – as a matter of fact more than 56 years – I have learned that networking is based on the stones we lay in front of us to walk our path of life, your life. My stepping stones that meant and still mean the most to my success in life, in networking are: faith, hope, trust, respect, integrity, empathy, perseverance, enthusiasm, success, failure, giving back, and love. In the following chapters, I will touch upon these and outline how they played a critical role in my networking life, on and off the streets, in and out of the military, and with success and failure in business. The words and their meanings have enabled me to be inspired, motivated, and enthused while inspiring, motivating, and enthusing others in my network.

Some of my character traits have to do with my underlying values, norms or belief system. Your character – all aspects of your behavior and attitude – make up your networking personality. Everyone has character traits and a behavior that is both good and bad – everyone!

Networking is your daily life. In networking you do things, you feel things, you hear things, you say things, and you think of things. From the moment you were born, you were networking. Just think of other people in your network that are already telling stories about you, about how cute you are, all the hair you have or the hair that you don't have, your big brown eyes, and of course your name. Like many others, my name, Charles Douglas Armando, was given to me by my parents. They wanted to give respect to their network by naming me after someone dear to them.

Charles was the name of my mother's favorite brother, who became my Godfather after I was baptized. Baptism in my Christian faith means thanking God for his gift of life. My parents made a decision to let my life begin on the journey of faith and therefore asked for the Church's support. That journey of faith involves turning away from all that is evil, turning towards Jesus, and becoming a member of the local and worldwide Christian family.

Douglas was the name of my mother's favorite film star, Douglas Fairbanks Jr. He was quoted as saying: "*I was only saying to the Queen the other day how I hate name dropping.*" Now I know why my mother gave me that name. That remark sounds like something I could have said to the people in my network!

Armando was the name of my father's favorite brother, who stood in for me at my Confirmation. Confirmation in my Christian faith means accepting responsibility for your actions and destiny. From my Confirmation, I received a special grace by which my faith was deepened and strengthened. It would be strong enough not only for my own needs, but also for the needs of others with whom I would try to share.

Networking is taking a walk, running, jumping, or just sitting down drinking a cup of coffee while you think about your life and the lives of others in your network. I can honestly say that you always network, and yes, even while you are dreaming, or gazing away. Everyone has dreamt something, woken up and told others about it, or called someone to explain what their dream was about. What about those dreams have you waking up and feeling bad or sad? Welcome to networking in the living color! We all have these moments in our networking lives. We have to build in the trust, faith, and hope that things will get better. You are in the driver's seat and no one else. If things are not going as well as you wanted or hoped for, then look in the mirror and do a self-reflection networking session. Ask someone dear to you in your network to listen to your network stories. For me it's my wife, Herma, whom I have been married to for more than 33 years. She is who I turn to to bring and share my networking stories, worries, disappointments, frustrations, joy, excitement, and love. This girl has gone a few rounds with me in the ring of life, that sometimes had me thinking about throwing the white towel.
Originally, this probably is related to tossing up the white flag; something that also indicates surrendering in battle or facing defeats in life. Most of us will recognize this from boxing when the coach of a boxer throws a white towel into the ring to give the signal that the fight is over, and that the boxer is going to give up or surrender. Believe me; we all have to take defeats in life. When you do, think of what Muhammad Ali said once:

"I never thought of losing, but now that is happened, the only thing is to do it right. That's my obligation to all the people who believe in me."

I hope everyone has someone whom they can call their friend; a friend that listens and can see where and what you are doing in the correct fashion. Someone that has a genuine concern for your well-being, and someone that knows that deep in your heart and soul you want and try to do things right and honestly. Networking is putting your character into action by your behavior toward yourself and others. Your actions demonstrate to others in your network who and what kind of a person you are. They show your true character in your behavior to have faith or no faith at all, to have hope or be hopeless, to be trustworthy or untrustworthy, to be respectful or disrespectful, to be friendly or angry, to be happy or sad, to be quiet or nosey, to be honest or dishonest, to be optimistic or pessimistic, to be giving or greedy, to be a shy person who tends not to socialize much, or a person that seems to be a natural networker. Remember, networking is life, your life, and actions speak louder than words. Just listen to *"Your Wake-Up Call"* when it comes, and don't put ear plugs in or turn the music up to drown out your character call.

There are many words, or lists of words that people would like or want to see in someone's character. In fact, if you and I were each to make our own list of character traits, it's likely that these would be somewhat different. Please understand that I'm only going to touch upon some of the character traits that others say I possess and ones that other people in my network have seen in my behavior. There are more, but I took the ones I think will make the difference in networking. These character traits have enabled me to build my network based on gaining the trust of others and earning their respect while giving back to others. They are what my character is built upon and allow me to give a *"Wake-Up Call"* to both the rich and famous, or the poor and unfamiliar people in my network. These character traits are the inspirational, motivational, and enthusiastical elements and factors for me to get up every day with hope and faith in what is going to come.

Sometimes, different words might be used to describe the same character traits. Here, in bold, I show you the words associated with each chapter in my book that you are reading right now. Next to the bolded words are the other words I could have used or may come to your mind while reading the chapter heads:

Values or Ethics
Norms or Beliefs
Character or Personality
Behavior or Demeanor
Faith or Conviction
Respect or Admiration
Integrity or Honesty
Empathy or Sympathy
Perseverance or Persistence
Enthusiasm or Energy
Success or Achievement
Failure or Defeat
Networking or Connections
Giving Back or Generosity
Love or Charity

Your list may contain character traits that I didn't think about and would have included if I had thought of them. You may have included some words in your list that others would not agree with. I might include "intelligence" in my list of character traits, but you might say that intelligence is not a character trait but an ability. In the full knowledge that there may be other lists of character traits just as valid, I am touching on my most important ten character traits that have been very helpful to me in networking. Character traits that have been my guide for keeping me inspired, motivated, and enthused in life.

In the following chapters, I will also explain how these ten most important character traits have played a vital role in my life. I think it's important to narrow down your character traits, because they demonstrate or show who you are and what you stand for. They are the basics of your values and norms system; a system that started the moment you were born and continues to develop throughout your networking life to a point of maturity.

My ten character traits I keep deep in my heart and try daily to display are:

faith, hope, trust, respect, integrity, empathy, perseverance, enthusiasm, giving back, and love.

I always preach that old saying: "actions speak louder than words." It is very true when it comes to networking. In networking you can see the true character of other people, and their behavior will demonstrate what is truly in their hearts. You learn about who people are and what their character traits are by watching how they interact in networking settings and by paying attention to how they treat and interact with others.

BEHAVIOR

Behavior is defined as the manner in which one behaves; the actions or reactions of a person in response to external or internal stimuli.

I can tell you that claiming and being "The NetworKing" has affected and developed my manner in which I approach others in my network. It has caused me to behave or react much differently to situations and circumstances than before. From the moment people see on my business card that I'm a professional networker, the Founder of The NetworKing Academy, I trademarked the word "The NetworKing," my company's name is "The NetworKing Corpora tion," and I label myself "The NetworKing" – a King of Networking – they are amazed that I could turn a word into a business.

38

They even introduce me to others in their network as "The NetworKing" and state that if there's is someone that acts, behaves, and emulates networking, it's "the Rufman." This is a wonderful complement to receive from others in my network. They branded my character and behavior.

I have branded "The NetworKing" in such a way that when the word, idea, or image appears in the market, more and more people will identify the word "networking" to me. Through the brand "The NetworKing," I'm identified as a motivator and inspirator who can energize and excite a room full of people, or just an individual having one of those days. Not only did I build a brand that is recognizable, but I also have tried to build a good reputation that is based on trust and respect while giving back to others in my network. Believe me, everyone is a networker. It's just that I coined the word and phrased and turned it into a brand and business.

With fast moving technology, I also started to use the Internet to help in building my reputation as well as expanding The NetworKing brand worldwide. In Chapter 8, "NetworKing in the Modern World," I will tell you more about how I use the worldwide web as a marketing tool in order to make a successful brand even stronger.

Writing a book is also a very good way to build your reputation. A couple of years ago, I wrote my first book *"Network Your Way To Success,"* in English, and it sold so well, worldwide that it became a "Bestseller." Knowing this fact, I decided to get it translated into Dutch.
I had a lot of people in my network asking and wanting to translate my book into Dutch, but I was not ready. I just didn't feel I had the right person for the job until I met Anne Marie Westra-Nijhuis from the town, Enschede, in the Netherlands. Anne Marie has values and norms very similar to mine, and she has an impeachable character and unwavering behavior. After meeting and doing successful business with Anne Marie, I decided that she would be the person to translate my book into Dutch. This was one of my best business decisions I have ever made. Within three months, she transla-

ted my book and we were able to publish it. The Dutch edition was also an addition to my English book with stories and an update on my networking activities. The name of my Dutch book is *"Netwerk Je Weg Naar Succes."* What a great title; its original, don't you think? By the way, my Dutch book became a "Bestseller" too. Now, I'm working on getting the Chinese translation into the ranks of a "Bestseller." Too bad that Anne Marie doesn't speak Chinese!

Did I ever tell you how I met Anne Marie? I met her at a business conference in Rotterdam, the Netherlands, where I was a Keynote Speaker. I will never forget that day, because it led to a very close cooperation with Anne Marie. Over the years, she has become my very dear friend and only business partner. Besides translating my book, *"Network Your Way To Success,"* into Dutch, she also arranges all my networking trainings, lectures, workshops, and maintains my Social Media platforms. Further she is the Co-Founder of The NetworKing Academy and keeps me "out of trouble" – as we say on the street. She has my back, or in the military she would take a bullet for me. Anne Marie feels much honored that I placed her name on the front cover of my Dutch book, and she is very privileged to have this close business partnership with me. And you know what? I feel privileged to work so closely with Anne Marie too!

Back to the business conference in Rotterdam, Anne Marie had recently started her company, EPLÚ Management Support, and entered into the business arena as an entrepreneur. By participating at the conference – she had to make a two and a half hour trip from her hometown, Enschede, to Rotterdam – she was expecting to gain a lot of knowledge and to become inspired, motivated, and enthused.

I'm glad I have been able to be part of meeting the high expectations of hers by ending the day for her with an inspiring, motivating, and enthusiastic session about networking. All the inspiring speakers at the business conference proved to be the cream of the crop for her, but the one that most impressed her was "Charles Douglas Armando Ruffolo, professional networker, trainer, international speaker, author and publisher" as the announcement stated. She thought: *"This American networking guru, known as "The NetworKing," who had been living off and on in the Netherlands for over 25 years, personally shook hands with everyone at the entrance .Wow, that was very promising!"* Later on she said: *"Dutch and sober minded, I became enthralled with this "American show." What a passionate speaker!"*

My style of presenting and lecturing is often very unusual to most of the people attending my sessions because I tell it like it is in a quite natural way. My lectures, workshops, and training sessions are also very interactive and are marked by a flamboyant and elaborate performance that gives a colorful display and unique behavior on the values and norms of networking. I never stay on stage or at the podium; I always get off my soapbox and go into the audience or the crowd.

People do not fall asleep or appear bored to death. They do laugh at my explanations with expression of my networking stories. I get the crowd or audience pumped up, inspired, excited, enthused, and motivated about networking by empowering them. Their time with me is time well spent, fun, enlightening, and educational. It's my way of making and energizing to others in my network a memorable performance, and that they will leave there thinking and remembering "The NetworKing." I always say: "I'm just planting a seed of networking in your minds, so that next time when you hear the word networking, you will think of Charles Douglas Armando Ruffolo, the Rufman!"

Like the title of this book, *"Your Wake-Up Call,"* I will make sure that you are inspired, motivated, and enthused about yourself and ready to energize your network. I base my in-depth knowledge, learned skills and success plus failure on my networking stories to gain the respect and attention of my audience. I only talk about what I know, tell them the whole story, and nothing but the truth about networking. Just like you, I'm in charge of my networking stories, and they are my own personal stories. I bring them across gracefully and with confidence.

My stories capture the audience because they are real, believable, and worthwhile to listen to and to read. Networking is not an act! Your networking stories must capture the attention of others in your network.

For example, during my lecturing sessions I ask the public to raise their hands if they want to make money. Of course everyone is there to do business, and I get a lot of raised hands. Some people keep their hands lowered because they think they are not there to make money and just to give it out. I try to get people to understand that in business you have to make money. This is the key to keep your business afloat. Please don't get me wrong. I didn't say that I love money, but I see money as an instrument that acts as a medium of exchange in transactions or facilitates trade and services.

If we did not have this instrument called money, we would be reduced to an economy and market based on bartering when trading goods or services. Without the exchange of money, every item you want to purchase has to be exchanged for something that another person could provide. For example, a mechanic needs to find a farmer whose tractor needs repairing, so he can trade his skills for food, like eggs, or milk for a tune-up or oil change. What if the farmer's tractor does not need to be fixed, or if a farmer cannot give the mechanic any more eggs than the mechanic could reasonably use?
Fin-ding specific people to trade with makes it very difficult to specialize. People might starve before they were able to find the right person with whom to barter.

With money, however, you don't need to find a particular person. You just need a market in which to sell your goods or services using money as the means of exchange or trade. In the market, you don't barter for individual goods; instead you exchange your goods or services for a common medium of exchange — that is, money. You can then use that money to buy what you need from others who also accept the same medium of exchange.

Anne Marie was one of the first ones I saw bravely raising her hand on my question who wanted to make some money. As I needed two "victims" to make this exercise work, I called her and another person to come forward and gave her and the other person the opportunity to introduce themselves to the public. Then I asked them to help me keep an eye on my time. I always do this exercise, because it helps to keep me on track with the amount of time I have to speak. In this case, I told the other person that she could earn 5 Euros if she would be my time keeper and let me know out loud when I had five minutes left in my lecturing time.

Anne Marie would be my back-up time keeper by holding the 5 Euros. If the first time keeper was one second early or later then I would get 10 Euros from her, and Anne Marie would keep the 5 Euros she was holding. This way, I wouldn't only have an eye kept on my time, but I also would make some money. Anne Marie and her colleague time keeper accepted the terms and conditions of our deal, but not everyone ended up being happy. I lost 5 Euros, the time keeper won, and Anne Marie got nothing. Yep, you can't have it all!

Anne Marie performed so well that it gave me networking grounds to call her "my friend" at the exit; where I shook the hands again of everyone leaving the room.

A few days later, she decided to send me an email and put her new-found knowledge directly into practice. She really paid attention when I talked about the skills of "how to stay in people's minds." Therefore, her email to me was actually full of my own words. She was inspired, motivated, and enthused about doing business, as I was to have her in my network. This is what she wrote to me on the 16th of June in 2009:

Dear Mr. Ruffolo,

Herewith I would like to thank you for your inspiring keynote session du-. ring Onebizznessday on Friday 12th June last. I was one of your "victims" who was asked to step forward and speak! And so I did, as you would remember definitely. When I left the room at the end of the session, you even called me "a friend." I was also the one you borrowed the 5 Euros to, that I could earn definitely when I would be the first one to say: "Mr. Ruffolo, 5 minutes left." Unfortunately I had to give them to my "fellow entrepreneur." But I had been in a position to give you my business card. By the way, I did not receive yours, but as you taught me: "It doesn't matter who you know, but who knows you!"" Networking = making connections between similar groups of people. Keep it simple; it doesn't have to be so complicated" you said. So, Mr. Ruffolo, would you be surprised when I told you that I started my career as a 2nd Lieutenant in the Dutch army for 4 years? Thanks again for the inspiration. Last but not least, I herewith would like to order your book "Network Your Way to Success," and I would be honored if you would write a personal note in it. Thanks in advance and awaiting your early reply.

Kind regards,

Anne Marie Westra, "Entrepreneur"'!

But there was a sneaky note at the end of her message:

"If you think I am only writing you to say thanks, you are wrong. I am writing you to do business! So if you know anyone in your network that is looking for an executive professional, I shall be very glad to hear from you. On my website – www.e-plu.nl – you will find all the information you need."

I answered her with this email:

Anne Marie,

Thanks for your email and it's terrific to see that you are effectively "Networking." YES, I remember you well and which years and where were you stationed in the Dutch Military? You can order my book, by going to the ordering page on my website – www.thenetworking.com – and of course I will write something in the book for you! Hope to see you "Networking" in the market and stay focused on energizing your "Network."

Later, Ruf

Anne Marie answered:

Dear Mr. Ruffolo,

Thank you for your reply. I just ordered your book and I very much appreciate it that you are willing to write something in it for me. I started my career in the Dutch Military, where I worked as a "KVV-officer" (in Dutch: "Kort Verband Vrijwillger") for four years. I started with a military training in Middelburg at OCMA (I believe this is currently situated in Bussum or Hilversum). After that I was stationed in Deventer at Staff NLC (National Logistic Commando), where I worked as a lieutenant executive assistant for Chief of Staff for 2 years. Then, I was stationed in Apeldoorn at Staff 1LK (First Army Corps), also as a lieutenant executive assistant for Chief of Staff. At that time, I also joined international military exercises in Germany, where I actually learned the "military" ropes. I could not imagine a better start of my career than these "Dutch Military" years. If I had to do it over again, I certainly would make the same choice. And talking about networking: in LinkedIn I found the daughter of the general I worked for in Apeldoorn. And guess what, she just asked me if I would be interested in helping

45

organizing 3 international conferences. You are so right by saying: "Networking enables you to go directly from A to Z and skip the usual path through B to Y!" Thanks again and looking forward to receiving your book.

Kind regards,

Anne Marie Westra

"Networking does enable you to go directly from A to Z and skip the usual path through B to Y." Thanks to the fact that we had something immediately in common – we both had a military background – it all went into rapid fire change from that moment on. With subsequent participation of Anne Marie to The Network Club Winter Event at the Hilton Hotel in Amsterdam, it served as the beginning of a great partnership.

So you can imagine that I'm very proud to have announced on my website that, "In 2010, Charles Ruffolo, The NetworKing, entered into partnership with Anne Marie Westra from EPLÚ Management Support, project & event manager, communications professional and marketer. Charles and Anne Marie jointly organize networking training, workshops, presentations and lectures for companies, groups, and organizations throughout the Netherlands and beyond. Charles's book, "*Network Your Way to Success*," his Guide to the Power of Networking, was translated into Dutch by Anne Marie, under the title, "*Netwerk Je Weg Naar Succes.*"

For a couple of years now, Anne Marie and I have also bundled up our strengths on stage to lecture on "*Network Your Way in the Social World.*" Based on my five basic principles of networking, I motivate people on how to effectively network by using the tools they already have. By using her own personal experiences, Anne Marie shows the audience how to use these same tools in the social world to market, advertise and promote yourself, your company, or your product. As you can't network without giving back, we decided that once a year we will give our workshop to support the Dutch Fight Against Cancer charity.

Anne Marie and I continuously further strengthen our partnership. So it won't surprise you that she played an important role in editing and translating this book "*Your Wake-Up Call.*" When I look into the future, I am very excited about the grand and wonderful things that have yet to happen. As I always say, "I don't believe in "being lucky" or "being in the right place at the right time." On the contrary, I contend that people to whom good things happen usually have set themselves up to succeed!

Before jumping onto Chapter 3, "Faith & Hope," let me tell you another one of my networking stories that didn't turn out so well because of my character and behavior that brought shame and dishonor to myself and my family. Being the youngest in a large family, my siblings would always tell me what to do and what not to do, who to hang around with, and who not to be seen with. My brother Johnny (everyone called him The Hawk or Hawky- John) told me to stay away from this one particular guy. By the way, Johnny is the one that labeled me "Bone-Yard" or "The Bone;" an expression he coined to refer to my chest looking like a grave yard of bones (I was very skinny when I was young).

You could count each and every bone from my ribcage, and still today my brothers and sisters would call me "Bone- Yard." Don't you even think of using it now… it's a nickname only for my siblings to use! Hawk told me to stay away from this guy and not to loaf or be with him, because he was not honest, trustworthy, and he was not part of the family. As a young 12 year old wayward boy, I didn't always listen very well. One day, we were loafing on the 4th Street corner and this guy came up to me and asked what I was doing.

I said that I was just hanging out, and waiting for something to do or happen. Then he said he had an idea for some excitement and asked if I wanted to drive around with him. Of course I said yes, because I was just hanging out on the corner, doing nothing. So I jumped into his car and we drove around just talking crap to each other when he suddenly said: "Let's break into a gas-station for some fun." My first thought was that it wasn't cool and why would I want to break into a gas station for some fun? I thought it was fun just riding around the streets. He had a few good reasons, and he knew a gas station that was very easy to break into. We could take the things and sell them on the market to make some money. So I said, "OK: let's do it."

He drove up the hill and stopped at a gasstation which was closed. He parked the car in the back; we got out, broke the back window, and climbed into the gas station. We took tools, oil, and anything that we could carry. It was only equipment; no cash. When we got out of the gas station, I told him I didn't want anything out of the stuff, nor money for it, and that I would start walking home. I told him it was fun and said thanks for the exciting adventure. Then I left, and he drove off down the street. I never heard from him again, until one day when I returned from playing basketball. My sister told me that the police were in the house talking to my father, and that I was in really big trouble... again!

Trouble did not do it; I did. I had broken into a gas station, and the other guy was caught for selling stolen goods and would go to jail. My father called me into the kitchen where the Police Officer was, and told me that he would ask me one simple question only one time and that I better be honest and not lie. He asked me: "Did you break into the gas station with this other guy?" I quickly looked into the eyes of my father and I knew it would be better for me not to lie and face the consequences head on. Just the look on my father's face already scared me like nothing before. The Police Officer looked like Mother Theresa compared to my father's facial expression and body language. "*YES SIR,*" I said, and my father looked at the Police Officer who quickly replied: "Joe, he is yours and I trust you will handle your boy your way and the correct way." As the Officer left, I was hoping and praying that he would take me with him. I felt I would have been in better hands in the custody of the Officer, than in my father's hands!

I won't tell you all what happened after that incident. For the next six months, I paid the price for my stupid behavior. I remember very well my father saying to me: "Son, how could you steal from someone else?" To top it off, he said: "Do you have any idea how much shame, disrespectfulness, and dishonor you brought to our family? Your brother even told you not to hang around or do anything with that guy. Why did you not listen to him? Oh you are going to pay the price for that boy!" I hurt badly inside and of course outside for many months, if not years to come. I showed a side of my character that did not reflect the character my parents instilled in me or the behavior of our family. I showed a lack of honor and respect for others and my actions dishonored the family and our reputation. Therefore I had to make it up by apologizing in person to the owner and others in the family. I was punished to many months of hard work!

At the young age of twelve, I learned a few new things about life. The first was that you could be forgiven for your behavior, but not forgotten. The second was like my father said: "Bad company ruins good morals." The third was that we had members in our family whose name wasn't Ruffolo, Sorrentino, Garritano, Welsh, or Bongartz, but who were still in our family. OK, not really in our immediate family, but in "The Family," if you know what I mean!

At the end of this Chapter 2, we have learned that a strong character and good behavior will prepare us for effectively networking and take what life has to give. As the next two lines of the song read: *"Looking for adventure, In whatever comes our way."*

"All you have in life is your reputation: you may be very rich, but if you lose your good name, then you'll never be happy. The thought will always lurk at the back of your mind that people don't trust you. I had never really focused on what a good name meant before, but that night in prison made me understand."
Sir Richard Branson

CHAPTER 3

FAITH & HOPE

"You will not enter paradise until you have faith. And you will not complete your faith until you love one another."
Prophet Muhammad

FAITH

Faith is belief with strong conviction; firm belief in something for which there may be no tangible proof; complete trust in or devotion to. Faith is the opposite of doubt.

Lifelong experience has taught me that networking is based on keeping the faith and hoping that things will work out for you. You will get the break you are looking for, the job position will become available for you, and what you have been working so hard on will turn into success. Others in your network will recognize your talent and skills and therefore want you in their network. You need to follow a built-in guiding system that keeps you inspired, motivated, and enthused in good times and bad times during success and failure in your life. This is one of the many reasons why I wrote this book. Therefore I hope it will guide you to keep the faith and hope in yourself and your network.

Do you have the faith to believe in yourself? Do you have the faith to believe in others, a family member, a friend, your business partner, or your network? I believe we all do, but sometimes we are just scared to be confronted with that. So the question is; how much faith do we allow until it becomes reality in our life? Your actions are a critical part of faith and they demonstrate your true colors. Faith is in action when you make yourself vulnerable... practicing what you preach, or believe.

Close your eyes and visualize what you are thinking about or hoping for. Do you see it? Do you see yourself scoring that winning goal? Do you imagine it's the final minute of a basketball game, your team is down by 2 points, and the play is made that you get the ball with four seconds left on the clock? At every practice session this exercise is drilled into you and your teammates. At the four second mark you are positioned in the right corner of the court to shoot the 3 point jump shot. In your mind you have gone over this a thousand times, and you have the faith and hope that you are going to win the game with this 3 point conversion. Or you have faith that things are going to work out, only at this very moment; you just don't know how you are going to handle it. Deep down in your heart and soul, you know it will happen. Even though you don't have the evidence right now, it will be successful and you will get what you hoped for.

Having faith in networking is a learned behavior that could produce a strong conviction or emotionally rewarding kind of trust in yourself and in that of other people in your network. Faith in networking is the kind of trust that you enter into with your whole being. Therefore we must realize that, when faith has been broken, it really hurts deep inside, and that it may take away your inspiration, motivation, and enthusiasm. Faith is also the kind of trust that finds a way to trust again; despite the hurt. You learn to regain the faith in yourself and in others, and you will try to understand why someone in your network has broken that trust. You search for the good in your network. Are you already fired up to be more inspired, motivated, and enthused about yourself and others in your network?

Faith is the ability to trust something from the very core of your being. Being bounded together by trust touches the deepest aspects of who we are, and we hope that everyone possesses those same aspects. We are living in a faith based world that inspires us to be everything we can be. When faithful people not only hold the trust they place in others but also hold the trust that others place in them, then it will become one of the most important aspects of their human existence.

A network is a collection of people who share the same value system, have similar character traits, respect, and believe in each other. It's a community of people who have made the commitment to trust one another, to care for each other's spirits, souls, businesses, dreams and hopes, and are a form of faith that serves the purpose of helping each other.

You know when you hear and see someone in your network who displays true faith in something; a faith that is sometimes blind and requires only body and soul neglecting the mind and the spirit.

So if we understand that faith in networking is a positive emotion we need, then we will also understand the opposite of faith; doubt. It is with doubt that we and others in our network begin to question our faith in something and start wondering why for example we are not successful. Doubt is a negative but very powerful emotion that effectively blocks the creative process. It is opposing faith and creating a belief that we're not good networkers, or we don't have a powerful network.

On the other hand, faith is the energy, the enthusiasm, and the power behind our networking ability to attract others in our network and everything we ask for effortlessly. We have to rely on our faith, even when everyone else tells us we are crazy, we will not succeed, or when there is no evidence what-so-ever that we will reach that point.

Faith means nothing more than a belief; a thought about something, someone, or some situation that cannot be proven. It's one of your key elements to your success in life, your life, and the lives of others in your network. Essentially, faith is no tangible evidence for what you know will help prove what you think, want, or pursue. Faith will only back up or support your claim, idea, theory, or thought. Faith is simply an overwhelming understanding convincing you what you hoped will be reached, achieved and sustained. Faith keeps me inspired, motivated, and enthused in all types of circumstances and situations that I'm faced with daily.

HOPE

Hope is to cherish a desire with anticipation, to desire with expectation of obtainment, or to expect with confidence.

When I think of hope, I always think of what President Clinton said to me when I hosted him in 2004 during an event for my Giving Back Foundation (more about my Giving Back Foundation you can read in Chapter 9, "Giving Back & Love"). After his speech and readings from his book *"My Life,"* that at that time just had been launched, he took questions from the Giving Back students in the audience. Janet Abdelatif, one of the Giving Back students, was taught the five values of Giving Back: Hope, Respect, Responsibility, Enthusiasm and Generosity. She asked President Clinton this question: "President Clinton, one of the values of Giving Back is Hope. You were born in Hope, Arkansas, what does Hope mean to you?" President Clinton answered by saying:

"It means that, first of all, Hope is a state of mind, it is a decision you make every day. And I want to emphasize that because. . . hope is not something that you sort of have or don't have. You have to make a decision about how you are going to look at every day and I learned that from my mother. My father was killed in a car wreck before I was born; my mother's second husband was an alcoholic, who beat her until I got big enough to stop him.

54

My mother was married five times to four men and three of them died on her. She had a lot of problems, but she got up every day with the expectation, that something good was going to happen. And she could make something good happen and how she thought of her life was a choice! So hope to me is the belief that today can be better than yesterday, and tomorrow can be better than today. And no matter what happens to your life, it is still a gift, because you might feel very bad about someone your age or younger died today in a way that was completely unfair and completely unfortunate. In the roulette wheel of life someone was taken away and you're still here. Therefore it is cynical and selfish to live without hope. That is what I believe."

I believe the same thing. Throughout our lives we are faced with situations that are considered either good or bad. How we react to these situations is based on our value system or how we are programmed. Take for example my very good friend, Joseph Oubelkas, who was sentenced to ten years in prison for something he didn't do. In his book, "*400 brieven van mijn moeder,*" (400 letters from my mom) you can read how Joseph survived 4.5 years imprisonment – 1367 days and nights – by using the values and norms that were taught to him by his parents. He held onto the characteristics that his mother continued to feed and nurture him from afar: faith, hope, trust, respect, empathy, love, and a remarkable demonstration of perseverance.

In his book, Joseph describes how during the harsh and unjust life in various prisons, he was unconditionally supported by thousands of letters and cards from friends, acquaintances, and strangers. Most importantly he was supported by the 400 letters from his mother. These letters inspired, motivated, and enthused him to keep the faith:

"Life, my child, has many barriers you must cross. Most of the time, you will be warned. But everyone stumbles once in their life on an invisible barrier. Then, my son, you must stand up and move on for you will see be-

tween the darkest clouds, a heavenly blue, and flowers blooming in their full beauty. Lots of love, Mom"

Joseph freed himself by physically being in a box, but not doing what others wanted or thought he had to do. During a conference in the Netherlands in May 2012, where Stedman Graham and Joseph were both speaking – Joseph is a frequent speaker and lecturer now – Stedman told him that: *"Freedom is about a way of thinking. Freedom is about understanding you can do anything that you want. Freedom is about being able to take information and education and make it relevant to your own growth, every single day. Freedom is not staying in the box. Freedom is not doing what other people want you to do."*

When Joseph was asked about the worst part of being locked up, he answered: *"The worst part was knowing I was there unjustly and how easy it was to put someone behind bars without any sort of evidence. This just wasn't possible, but still it happened! Those thoughts went through my mind constantly."*

These impressive words echo like Dr. Martin Luther King Jr, an American Civil Rights leader, in his open letter, *"The Negro Is Your Brother,"* written on April 16th 1963 while he was in Birmingham Jail. It stated: *"Injustice anywhere is a threat to justice everywhere. We are caught in an inescapable network of mutuality, tied in a single garment of destiny. Whatever affects one directly, affects all indirectly..."*

I would strongly recommend you to read Joseph's book, and if you ever have the opportunity to watch Joseph speak, do it! Joseph also has a website: www.oubelkas.nl.

Faith deepens your relationships with others and enables you and others in your network to fully explore the meaning of who you are while capturing the beauty of each other's lives. Hope is an encouragement not to overlook the many good and positive aspects of your networking life and be prepared to take calculated risks to reach your goals in your daily life. Remember I said calculated risks mean that you have to weigh the consequences of putting your faith and hope in something or someone at all times.

As we have witnessed in this chapter, faith and hope keep us focused on making things happen and embracing networking as it comes. We sing the next verse of the song, *"Yeah, darlin' gonna make it happen, Take the world in a love embrace."*

"And so I tell you, keep on asking, and you will receive what you ask for. Keep on seeking, and you will find. Keep on knocking, and the door will be opened to you. For everyone who asks, receives. Everyone who seeks, finds. And to everyone who knocks, the door will be opened."
Jesus Christ (Luke 11:9-10)

CHAPTER 4

TRUST & RESPECT

"I know God won't give me anything I can't handle. I just wish he didn't trust me so much."
Mother Teresa

TRUST

Trust is the firm belief in the reliability, truth, ability, or strength in someone or something.

Trust has a major part in the foundation of establishing a network. If you put the effort of trust building in your network, there is a big chance that you might find success. Trust is heartwarming and a great attribute, but unfortunately it is also abused and broken by people. We learn to trust as we learn to love. Basic trust is the foundation of identity and self- trust enabling one to form trustful relationships throughout life, in marriage, with children, with society, and with our faith.

Trust in someone or something gives you hope. Trust does not make you afraid of the future; it helps you to be inspired, motivated, and enthused to reach your goals and objectives.

Probably the most important step to lay a solid networking foundation is building trust based on doing what you say you will do. At least try doing it with a genuine intention to fulfill the trust. Even if it's a small thing, canceling or failing to follow through will create hairline fractures within trusting others in your network. It will cause your foundation to crumble over time.

Trust is built and maintained by many small actions that you display to your network over time. Remember, it takes time to build trust and earn respect. I don't believe in giving someone the perception or the illusion that networking is fast, quick, and easy. It takes a lot of energy, effort, time, trials, and errors in networking to gain trust.

In our networking life, we put our trust in others to guide, support, lead, and tell us what to do and where to go. We put our trust in others to heal and even to love us. As we interact daily with others in our network in one way or another, we come to rely on each other for many things. We are taught to seek out others in our network for help. In a friendship we go to our friends, in our marriage we go to our spouse, and in our faith we turn to the one we rely on. What happens in your network when that person or persons you put all your trust into end up not being there for you or fails to help you? What happens when your significant other fails and can't emotionally, physically, medically, or spiritually support you anymore? What happens when your friends aren't there for you? What happens when that program you believed in comes to an end, and you are not completely healed? What happens when your human support is broken and you feel lonely? Believe me, this will happen in your life, and I hope that you calculate failure and disappointment. Everyone suffers betrayal and mistrust in their lifetime, and I mean everyone! It's one of the things we all have in common. When that happens, the trick is not to let it destroy your trust in others. I have the tendency to trust everyone, until they prove me different. I have learned the hard way in networking by not always listening to my gut feeling and the voice inside telling me not to go down that street, path, or do business with that person. The point is just don't let one experience of mistrust make you have misjudgments in handling other situations because that could damage you and harm others in your network.

When I was growing up in Pittsburgh, I remember I was running around with my friends from the 4th Street corner: Ikey, Shane, Eddy, Danny, Dino,

Tommy, and a couple of others. When someone was picking a fight with one of them, I immediately jumped in to help knowing and trusting that my back would be covered. I trusted that my friend Ikey would jump in to help me. Heck no! A few minutes later, when the other guy was getting the best of me, he ran away and left me there to get my butt kicked. After learning a very painful lesson, I finally crawled back to our 4th Street corner and asked Ikey where he was, why he ran away, and why he did not help me. I trusted that he would help me. After all, I was trying to help and protect him. Ikey answered that he didn't want to get beaten up too and trusted that I would get out of the situation. At 12 years old (Stage 2, Chapter 2, remember?) I quickly learned whom I could depend on and trust. I learned who would be there for me in good times and butt kicking times. Ikey and I have stayed very good friends to this day, and I know that if I would ever get in a fight again, he would be there for me… of course with his two boys now!

You know when you can trust someone in your network. You also know when you can't trust your network; you learn who to trust and who not to trust. Yet, what is trust, and how is trust usefully defined for you in your network? Can you build trust when it doesn't exist in your network? How do you maintain and build upon the trust you may currently have with your network? These are important questions for establishing, building, leading, communicating and giving back to your network. Trust has nothing to do with our rapidly changing world – trust was there from the beginning of time.

When trust exists in your network, almost everything will be easier and more comfortable to achieve. The chances of your success and the success of others in your network have become more achievable. Take a few moments to think of people in your network that you blindly trust, or people you surly don't trust. Now ask yourself: "Why do I trust them or why do I not trust them?" Keep listening to yourself, and look back to what that person did to gain your trust or to break that trust. You will get inspired, motivated, and enthused to do more things with people you trust than with people you don't.

Trust in yourself and others are valuable characteristics that I hope you will have, or obtain and keep.

In life you need to know quickly who you can trust, and the same goes for business. As I told you before, one of my strong points – and also my weak points – is that I trust people until they prove me differently. This characteristic sometimes gets me into trouble and causes me to lose money, waste time, and lose trust from others in my network. Once, I was eager to do business with someone in my network and several other people warned me to be very careful, because they heard and personally had bad experiences with this particular person. But with my enthusiasm and trust in people, I not only just pushed their advice aside; I also didn't follow my own feelings. My feelings were telling me to be very careful because the story that someone in my network was telling me was too good to be true. I would become a millionaire very easily by just energizing my network. Please realize that, if something sounds too good to be true, believe me it is! Exceptionally good friends told me to always test and investigate things and don't be fooled. Unfortunately, I didn't test and investigate this particular case. I was just thinking about this person going to turn me into a millionaire and of all the people I could help. So I ended up looking like a fool, but I can ensure you that that made me a much wiser person in life and business. I can tell from my own experience that the old expression: "At the end of the rainbow, there's a pot of gold," is NOT true. Our world population has reached seven billion people now and 15 - 20 million people are estimated to be millionaires. This is forecasted to rise to 38 million by 2020, but it only represents 0.2 - 0.3% of the world's population. So would you be surprised if I tell you that, although I am The NetworKing and personally know one of the world's richest people, Mr. Carlos Slim, I don't qualify to be in this percentage? Yes, I have followed and tracked down the rainbow many times but I came up empty handed. So if you ever end up in a situation like I just described; stop, think, and use the spirit you have – the spirit of a sound mind!

Trust is telling the truth – even when it is difficult – and being truthful, authentic, and trustworthy in your dealings with others in your network. Trust is when someone in your network believes your story. When you have believable stories that are dependable and reliable, people in your network will follow you. If your stories don't have trust, people will not believe your story and your network will crumble. You will not be invited to the party, get the heads-up on things, or get the internship for your child. Being honest and truthful is critical. It's a very important way to show your network who you are and what you stand for. And believe me, your network will only come to assist you and not leave you out in the dirt if they know your true colors. Your true colors are based on your values, norms, character, and behavior. Realize that trust is your internal clock that keeps on ticking no matter where you are, what you are doing, or who you are with!

As my very good friend, Stedman Graham, says: *"Everybody has 24 hours in a day and the question is, what you do with your 24 hours? That's what makes everybody equal."* I call this a *"Wake-Up Call"* for us all: trust matters every second, every minute, and every day in our lives!

RESPECT

Respect is a feeling of deep admiration for someone or something elicited by their abilities, qualities, or achievements.

You need to gain and earn the respect and admiration of others in your network by displaying adequate interpersonal or professional ability to effectively network. Being respectful is shown in a lot more ways than just saying "please" and "thank you." Remember, it takes respect to earn respect. I think everyone has heard or been taught the statement, "Respect your elders."

This means that we have to respect those that exhibit and proclaim knowledge derived from experiences that far surpass our own. The election of a tribal elder must be in accordance with the tribal rules stating that the previous elders nominate the new generation. The population has the final say in this matter.

Just like us, our elders were once young. They have memories of different fads, their first job, their first love, mistakes they have made, and things they have discovered. My point is they have stories to tell and things to teach us. They have lived through things that we ourselves can hardly imagine; for example, wars, depressions, occupation, slavery, and even life without computers or cell phones. They have lived through history and made history. They are amazingly strong, intelligent, and interesting human beings who have gone through real experiences. But generation to generation it seems like we are losing the respect for each other. I strongly recommend you try to live by the golden rule: *"Treat others the way you want to be treated."* People of that character are respectful.

I learned this from my parents and my Christian faith, but also by watching Sir Richard Branson. He put this into practice with his concept, *"The Elders,"* which originated from a conversation between Richard and his musician friend Peter Gabriel. The idea they discussed was simple; many communities look to their elders for guidance or to help resolve disputes. Could in an increasingly interdependent world, a "global village," with a small, dedicated group of individuals use their collective experience and influence to help tackle some of the most pressing problems facing the world today?

Richard Branson and Peter Gabriel took their idea of a group of "global elders" to the late Nelson Mandela, who agreed to support it. With the help of Graça Machel and Desmond Tutu, Nelson Mandela set about bringing *"The Elders"* together and formally launched the group in Johannesburg. In July 2007, *"The Elders"* represented an independent voice, not bound by the interests of any nation, government, or institution. They are committed to promoting the shared interests of humanity and the universal human rights we all share. They believe that in any conflict, it's important to listen to everyone no matter how unpalatable or unpopular this may be. They aim to act boldly, speaking difficult truths, and tackling taboos. They don't claim to have all the answers and stress that every individual can make a difference and create positive change in their society and in their network. *"The Elders"* is a form of giving back to their, not to our, network.

What a great initiative from Richard and Peter and a terrific way to give respect and seek wisdom from our elders! I was very proud and honored to support Richard Branson's program *"Virgin Unite"* that supports and funds *"The Elders,"* by organizing and arranging that Richard spoke in the Netherlands. Respect is what allows us to appreciate the best in other people in our network. Respect is trusting that all people in our network want the best for us. Within our value of respect, selfrespect is a vital ingredient, which results from knowing you have put forth your best effort. Your network is your life, your existence, your family, friends, and each person in your network has something to contribute. The secret is finding out who is the right person to effectively network with at the right time.

As Abraham Lincoln said in his speech in Clinton, Illinois on September 8, 1854: *"If you once forfeit the confidence of your fellow citizens, you can never regain their respect and esteem. It is true that you may fool all of the people some of the time; you can even fool some of the people all of the time; but you can't fool all of the people all of the time."*

I had heard that the Chinese are very respectful people and I have learned first-hand that this is absolutely true. You probably heard all the commotion about the size of the Chinese market and what is happening in China. The commotion that the Chinese are doing this, expanding there, taking over that, and being one of the largest markets. With approximately 1.29 billion people, China is the world's most populous nation in 2012, and China already stands as the second-largest economy in the world behind the United States.

Knowing this, I decided to get my book, *"Network Your Way To Success,"* translated into Chinese and bring it out on the Chinese market. I didn't want to wait for the Chinese market to come to me; I just went towards the Chinese. I energized my network and got my book translated, printed, and distributed in the People's Republic of China. In 2012, I even personally launched my book in Beijing. Launching my book in Beijing was an awesome experience, and I would like to give a special thanks to Lenard Wolters from Leonon Media, who was also responsible for publishing my English and Dutch book. Lenard had been launching his publishing business in China, and we decided to team up in Beijing. They say that the Chinese could be difficult to do business with, but let me tell you first-hand how I effectively networked my way to get my book published in China. It didn't cost me one cent or as the Chinese say not one Renminbi (the Renminbi is the official currency of the People's Republic of China)!

One day I was in my office at the World Trade Center at Schiphol Airport in Amsterdam, when my Chinese business associate, Lucien Tjon, who at that time was busy expanding "The NetworKing" concept in China, came into my office. Lucien brought an associate of his, who was studying in England and was working on finalizing her Master's degree in Finance & Accounting. She was with her parents, who traveled from Beijing to visit their daughter. Her parents didn't speak English or Dutch.
Lucien Tjon knew I train, lecture, and do a lot of business with the big four Accounting firms (PWC, Deloitte, Ernst & Young, KPMG). He wanted to see if I could help him find an internship in the United Kingdom for his associate at one of these firms. I quickly started turning the wheel of networking in my mind. I thought of whom I knew in these companies that knew me, because that is what networking is all about.

Because my Chinese business associate brought her to me, I told her I would help. Before I could help her, I asked her if she had ever read my book in English because I knew she had to be able to speak and read English due to her studying in the UK. When she said: "No, I haven't," like a fast gun-drawing cowboy, I immediately pulled out my book and gave it to her. I took aim, by writing something personal in it and then blew the smoke off the barrel by autographing it for her. Then she showed the book to her father, and with a lot of enthusiasm she told me that her father was a book publisher in China. At that point, my eyes got bigger and I was thinking how cool it would be to have my book translated in Chinese. I quickly thought how I am going to pull off this networking success story. . . "Charles Douglas Armando Ruffolo's book now translated in Chinese and available on the Chinese market!" This way, not only English and Dutch speaking people would read my book, but also the Chinese. Just think, Chinese people reading my networking story in their native language. Wow, how cool that would be! I was getting very inspired, motivated, and enthused about making this happen.

Now how could I craft this deal, right there, right now, before they would leave my office? Let's see, the young lady's father is a publisher and I am an author with a book that I know he would love to bring to the Chinese market. So I asked him if he was interested in publishing my book in China, and without any hesitation he said: "YES, of course" in Chinese. The translator repeated the "YES" in English. Now I had to learn to eat with chopsticks, because things started to move forward very quickly. I figured out that if I would help his daughter finding an internship and give him the rights to pu-blish my book, he would do it. We shook hands, and I pulled out a piece of paper to start writing down how we could further work this out.
Within one hour we had a working document to get started, and we signed the initial agreement that same day, before they left my office! We agreed that his daughter would work on the initial translation and then pass it over to a professional translator. As her father was eager to publish my book, I wan-ted to put a proposal together that would not only provide him with my net-working story but also absorbing all the costs. Guess what! He agreed to pay

67

for the translation, layout, printing, book registration, distribution, and marketing in China. The earning breakdown would be him getting 65% and me getting 35%, which I thought was a very good deal. I didn't have to put any money out for having my book in Chinese. Even if I wouldn't sell a ton of books, I had a great marketing tool and a new networking story that not too many people would be able to tell. Who do you personally know that has their book in Chinese?

Since 2012, my Book, "*Network Your Way to Success,*" is available in Chinese and here's the title:

交际 成功的摇篮

Pretty cool huh?

Before closing this chapter, I want to emphasize that although in most situations in networking – at work and in our life – trust and respect are linked closely together. I believe you must first build trust and from there you will earn respect with your deeds and actions. Just like the song continues to express these elements of networking with "*Fire all of your guns at once, and explore into space.*" Get ready to move to the next chapter, "Integrity & Empathy," while keeping inspired, motivated, and enthused about networking.

"If a man is respectful he will not be treated with insolence. If he is tolerant he will win the multitude. If he is trustworthy in his word his fellow man will entrust him with responsibility. If he is quick he will achieve results. If he is generous he will be good enough to be put in a position over his fellow men."
Confucius

CHAPTER 5

INTEGRITY & EMPATHY

"If a man is called to be a street sweeper, he should sweep streets even as a Michelangelo painted, or Beethoven composed music, or Shakespeare wrote poetry. He should sweep streets so well that all the hosts of heaven and earth will pause to say, "Here lived a great street sweeper who did his job well."
Martin Luther King Jr.

INTEGRITY

Integrity is the quality of being honest and having strong moral principles; moral uprightness.

Although we are born innocent, integrity is not something we have naturally. It is a value based on honesty and it will be developed over a lifetime.

Nowadays, more and more companies are looking for individuals with integrity to work for them or head their organizations. But look at the financial turmoil in the world right now. Isn't it because of a lack of integrity that all these things have happened?

Integrity means adherence to moral and ethical principles; soundness of moral character, honesty, and the state of being whole, entire, or undiminished as to morality.

It is doing what is right – legally and morally. Integrity is a quality you develop by adhering to moral principles. It requires that you don't do and say anything that deceives others. As your integrity grows, so does the trust others place in you. The more choices you make based on integrity, the more this highly prized value will affect your relationships with family, friends, and finally, the fundamental acceptance of yourself and how others accept you in their network.

Doing the right thing is an intangible quality that can only be measured through one's actions. However, those seemingly harmless actions have the potential to become something altogether different, so please remember that you can only lose your integrity once!

Integrity is also a character trait. It's the willingness to do what is right, even when no one is looking. It's the moral compass, the inner voice, the voice of self-control, and the basis for the trustimperative in networking.

Integrity is the ability to hold together and properly regulate all of the elements of a personality and your network. Persons of integrity, for example, are capable of acting on conviction within their network. Persons of integrity can also control impulses and appetites of others in their network. Integrity covers several other moral traits, and is indispensable for your ability to establish and maintain your network.

To have integrity is also to respect oneself as a human being. Persons of integrity never behave in ways that would bring themselves, their network, or the organization to which they belong or work for into disrepute.

When we put integrity on top of our networking list of values, we will become more responsible and accountable for our actions. I have learned throughout my networking life that we need guidelines and parameters on how we should relate with people in our network. Our actions reflect back to whom we are, which is a reflection of our family.

By learning and practicing integrity, we not only make our own lives better, but also improve the lives of everybody around us in our network, both now and in our future journey of networking. In networking we need to understand why we have rules, boundaries and expectations. We need to be reinforced and at some time experience the consequences of making the inappropriate or wrong choices. Integrity is a valuable characteristic to have in networking and one of our most important personal networking values. When integrity is compromised, memories will last very long. Defend your integrity as you would defend your life!

From a very young age, I have seen that integrity is visible in our daily lives. Growing up in Pittsburgh, Pennsylvania I have seen many things happening that, looking back now, bring up questions about the so called integrity of some of the people in my network. Just as society around them, these people were living and practicing integrity to its fullest. They complied with a code and the principles of integrity that were demanded from them. Later in my life, I found out that someone could live with integrity within their network, but to people outside their network they didn't show integrity.

I once knew a man who was a crooked businessman, but at home he was a wonderful father. I also knew a woman that cheated on her husband, but loved and cared very much for her children. We all have people in our network practicing different values of integrity that may be acceptable to us today, but tomorrow may be questionable. Both individuals in my example were not truly living or practicing integrity the way I see it, because if they did, they would have corrected their behavior in all walks of their lives. Everyone will experience this, in their life, and it may be hard to understand, but you must not forget that your behavior and that of others in your network is a constant re-examination of all aspects of our lives. You just have to find ways to free yourself from inappropriate or corrupt ideas, beliefs or behaviors that have snuck into your networking life, or get rid of these undesirable integrity characteristics that were once acceptable in your network, but have changed based on your own level of knowledge.

I have looked at my past on the streets, in the military, in business, and in my daily life in a rather critical eyeglass that is no way burning or punishing. It's one of learning the ways of life with integrity. I can tell you that, just because someone seems happy, a situation looks right, or a business comes across as successful, it doesn't mean that it has integrity. Integrity is determined by others in our network and our society we live and work in. I can honestly say that if I would cling to some of my old friends, my old ways, old mannerisms and so on, it would be very difficult or impossible for me to live in with their integrity, as I have moved on in my life. The manner we operated yesterday may not be acceptable today, and the fashion we do business today may not be totally acceptable in a different country or network.

In today's world it could be easy to get out of touch with reality and the truth and lose your integrity. Our lives are connected by rapidly changing technology (internet & social media) and our understanding of events, situations, and people evolve quickly. We have to hold firm and try not to jeapardize our integrity. I myself live in and keep my integrity by listening daily to many sources of news, reading books and newsletters that are out of the main stream, asking questions to others, discussing world situations, lecturing around the world, and picking up on life in the slow and fast lanes to stay up on the movement in the market. Most of all, I pray daily for guidance, wisdom, forgiveness, and truth.

EMPATHY

Empathy is the ability to understand and share the feelings of another.

Learning to relate to other people with empathy is very necessary in networking. Although some of us just naturally seem to be in tune with the feelings of our network, others might need a little help. Effective networking means always demonstrating empathy for others in your network and sharing your observations of others with your network, so that they learn to sense the feelings of others and will experience that others will be more responsive to them.

One of the main points of my books, my lectures, my workshops, and my training sessions is to empower others to what they already have: a powerful network that has hundreds if not thousands of people understanding and sharing their feelings. People often think they cannot relate to others because they are not in the same business, they don't have the same status, they don't drive the same expensive car, they cannot afford to eat in the same restaurant, or they aren't as successful as the others.

I use networking to inspire, motivate, and enthuse others; not to the status quo, but to the power of successfully energizing their network by teaching them that they were "Born to Network" and that they have to listen to their *"Wake-Up Call"* inside of them. Once you start listening to your network – and that does not just mean with your ears but also with your eyes, heart, and mind – you will better understand how easy it is to relate to others in your network. We have to break down those walls of unequal measurements of success and failure to realize that we are not the only one in the sinking boat or rising balloon. People often want to be in the networks of the famous people or the people that seem to be liked the most, you know those individuals who have thousands of friends or connections on social media. They are rooting for the favorite and not looking at the less known, unlike people.

I was always taught to root for "the underdog" instead of the favorite. I was taught to root for the one that was expected to lose or the one at a disadvantage. On the streets and at home, it was emphasized that you needed to put yourself in the shoes or place of others to better understand their situation. Coming from immigrant families and living in a very diverse community, we had other measures of success. That's why we would see people being successful, while others would not. To us, success was getting your high school diploma – even with very low grades, and getting a chance to compete in a context that you knew your chances of winning were slim. Possibly, getting into a fight with someone that for sure was going to knock you out or even put you in the hospital. Underdog or not, you could not back down; at least you had to try and keep the honor of your family name; a name of someone who was a fighter and survivor, not a loser or someone that backed down or gave up before trying. A true reflection of a person who could win the race, win the first place trophy, or beat the cramp out of the big guy. Pittsburgh, Pennsylvania, where I grew up, was a Blue-Collar city and a hard working steel mill town. Most of the people around town were called "Mill Hunky's," a disparaging reference to persons, especially laborers, from East-Central Europe. The term was also used to describe any mill worker, commonly referred to as Mill Hunky.

In that time, Pittsburgh's success was derived from the entrepreneurship and labor of its immigrants. Due to all the different ethnic backgrounds, we had our own lingo known affectionately as Pittsburghese. No one really knows where this came from. But much of it is a result of the ethnic mix of Pittsburgh, which is really a quintessential melting pot of the gateway to the west. We had Germans, Poles, Italians, Slovaks, Irish, and a dozen other nationalities that all were settled where the three rivers come together, in the valley, Mon Valley, from the *Monongahela Valley.* The word *Monongalia* is a Latinized version of the Native American word *Monongahela*, which means, "falling banks". It refers to the geological instability of the river's banks that surrounded the city of Pittsburgh. Did you know that Pittsburgh and the surrounding area was the home of Native Americans? For thousands of years, Native Americans (Paleo-Indians) inhabited the region, where the Allegheny and the Monongahela join to form the Ohio, perhaps as early as

19,000 years ago. And who said America wasn't old!

As I said, in our Pittsburgh culture, we had our special jargon, like "redd up" meaning tidy up your room. We used different words from different languages to get our message across to others in our network. I remember when I was a First Sergeant in the military, and I was conducting my routine inspection of the barracks. I was very upset because several rooms were not squared away. I called my Platoon Sergeants into my office uttering my enthusiasm, and no, it was not the type of enthusiasm you think; I was pissed off and yelling up a storm. I kept on saying: "You guys need to redd up this place" and they all looked at me and said: "First Sergeant, we understand the barracks are not clean enough, but what exactly are we going to do when we redd it up?" At that moment, I realized that I was using my Pittsburghese, which of course they couldn't understand.

We used other expressions like when the floor needed to be swept, we would pull out the "sweeper" (vacuum cleaner), or if I was using "dish soap" (dishwashing liquid) to wash the dishes. And of course our mailmen used "gum bands" (rubber bands) to bundle our mail, and I enjoyed an occasional "Ahrn" (Iron City beer). I remember getting a few snickers when I asked my Supply Sergeant for "rubbers" (galoshes – rubber boots) or when I asked for a "pop," a soft drink or soda. And let's not forget the most common Pittsburghese words, "Yinz" (you ones, you all), going somewhere and end questions with "n'at" (and that). I definitely drove Herma crazy and my soldiers in the military nuts with these and undoubtedly countless other Pittsburghese words and phrases. But I just thought these were the terms everyone used! Talking like this made you feel different, but also special.
There was one word I truly thought was Pittsburghese until I was stationed in Europe with the military, and that was the word "beaucoup."

I always thought that it was a special word for a lot of people, but when we were attending a busy event in Amsterdam and I said *"Man there are beaucoup people here,"* everyone looked at me and said that they didn't know that I spoke French!

Being raised with faith in an Italian/Irish environment made it easy to understand and share the feelings of another. As being Italians, we were seen as WOPs, an epithet used for Italian descent or US immigrants from the early 1900s. WOP stands for "With Out Papers." Many Italian immigrants had no papers to identify themselves and were branded WOPs. We were also called DAGOs, another offensive slur toward Italians who immigrated to the United States. DAGO comes from all the Italian workers who were paid as the "Day Goes," like modern "day laborers". But today, many Italian Americans will not be offended by these two slurs. The stories of others were used by our parents and environment to reinforce empathy and to motivate and inspire us to be all what we wanted to be and not to think that we couldn't become the champ or a king. We were taught to understand that if we would never give up, on any given day, we could be all that we wanted to be. We learned to relate to other people who had similar backgrounds or obstacles in their life and always root for the "underdog."

There were several underdog stories that were told and taught to us. Two of those stories impressed me most. It's the story of David & Goliath and the story of Rocky Balboa. The latter one, of course, is my most favorite, because I was young and could relate to the *"Italian Stallion!"* The stories go like this.

David and Goliath is a biblical story about David and the defeat of Goliath, the famous and fearsome Philistine warrior. A Philistine giant named Goliath, measuring over nine feet tall and wearing full armor came out each day, for forty days, mocking and challenging the Israelites to fight. David was an Israeli shepherd boy, who played the harp. David was not afraid of the giant's superior size, strength, and intimidating appearance. One day, David volunteered to fight against Goliath. Dressed in his simple tunic carrying

76

his shepherd's staff, slingshot, and a pouch full of stones, David approached Goliath. The giant cursed at him, hurling him threats and insults. He wore heavy armor and carried a long spear. David made a wise choice to shun the armor and utilized a slingshot, which he could fire from a distance. David executed his shot without flaw and without hesitation because he believed he was destined to win. As Goliath moved in for the kill, David reached into his bag and slung one of his stones at Goliath's head. The stone sank into Goliath's forehead; he fell face down on the ground, and was killed instantly. When the Philistines saw that their giant was defeated and dead, they turned and ran. Immediately David became a hero and everyone was extremely excited about his victory. So David, the underdog, who was the little shepherd boy, killed Goliath the giant and saved the Jewish people. No wonder David eventually became King of the Israelites!

Rocky Balboa was the *"Italian Stallion"* from Philadelphia who became an extremely infa- mous character in the Rocky series of movies. The films tell how an underdog, small time fighter could stand up to the heavyweight champion boxer, Apollo Creed, in the title fight. Rocky was a Southpaw fighter, and southpaw is a boxing term that designates the stance where the boxer has his right hand and right foot forward, leading with right jabs and following with a left cross right hook. Southpaw is the normal stance for a left-handed boxer. The Rocky series of movies – there are five of them – are a classic example of expounding on the underdog theme. Rocky takes on Apollo Creed and although he loses in the first movie, he does beat him in Rocky II. The rest of the series pits the *"Italian Stallion"* against various opponents he must struggle to defeat.

Once you feel or share the emotions of others, you begin to stimulate empathy for them. Empathy is something critical in networking. People may think it is the opposite of sympathy, but sympathy does not necessarily involve understanding, while empathy is the understanding of the emotional state of another individual. Sympathy means that you know how someone else feels, but you don't feel it. You can have sympathy for someone whose parent has died, but you may not actually feel the same grief.

Empathy means that you know how someone else feels and you also feel it. For example, if someone tells me about the difficulty of taking care of someone with cancer or tells me about problems they have getting out of a financial situation, I feel the same emotions as the other person is feeling because I experienced this myself.

Networking is not an intellectual pursuit but an expanded life experience that involves empathy. Your ability and willingness to put yourself in the other person's shoes or situation increases your ability to be successful. Learn to walk in the shoes of others within your network and emotionally understand their state of mind. I try to mirror my own experience with someone's emotions – happy, sad, nervous, joyful – because then I can really feel connected to that person. Remember, networking is finding what you have in common with others and feeling empathy for others. In networking, empathy is your silence conversation using your eyes, your heart, and your soul.

Having strong moral principles and truly understanding how others feel in your network will cause you to bring thunder and a bolt of lightning into your network. Just as the lyrics in the song say: "*I like smoke and lightnin',* *Heavy metal thunder.*"

"Leadership is about empathy. It is about having the ability to relate to and connect with people for the purpose of inspiring and empowering their lives."
Oprah Winfrey

CHAPTER 6

PERSEVERANCE & ENTHUSIASM

"If you live long enough, you'll make mistakes. But if you learn from them, you'll be a better person. It's how you handle adversity, not how it affects you. The main thing is never quit, never quit, never quit."
William J. Clinton

PERSEVERANCE

Perseverance is steadfastness in doing something despite difficulty or delay in achieving success.

One of the reasons I added this chapter part about Perseverance, is because Herma said that this is one characteristic that I really have to be aware of. That I have to be careful that it will not consume all my time and energy, take me off track, and drain my bank account and enthusiasm.

In our lives as in business we should possess perseverance – steady persistence in adhering to a course of action, a belief, or a purpose.

In networking, perseverance is the ability to adhere to a set of rules that enables you to reach your goal, regardless of the time devoted, the energy used, the effort applied, or the results achieved. Take for example your commitment, endurance, patience, and hard working towards setting up your company or studying to pass your school finals. Very often, people ask me: "how do you do it; how do you have the perseverance to be able to come across so calm and have everything under control?" I always reply by saying: "Well, it's easy; if you don't like something in your life, change it, because you are the only person who can change your own situation. If you are not getting the grades in school, then study harder. If you are not getting the job you think you should have, go find the right job. If you are not getting the clients, get off your butt and hit the streets." Besides the faith you have being prepared for ups and downs in life, you have to work hard to achieve the things in life and in your business that you want to achieve.

"But how do you stay so enthusiast towards life and networking?" they say. I say: "It's really not that difficult." "Why it is not so difficult? " "Well, whose life or business is it? It's your life, so bring excitement and fun into your life, job and business!" It always gets me when people live just for the weekends or for their vacations. As if life is only about the relaxing moments. Just think, there are 24 hours in a day, and if you break those hours down, it becomes clear that your life is going very quickly. I pointed out in Chapter 4 what Stedman Graham said about everyone having the same 24 hours in a day!

We have to get away from the mindset that networking is only for the wealthy or famous people. That these famous people are always inspired, motivated, and enthused in everything they do. They too need their *"Wake-Up Call."* Stop thinking you are the only one with issues or unique situations. Everyone is faced with challenges and obstacles in their life. We all have encountered what might be considered setbacks in our lives and also in work. But, please remember that you need to believe and understand that each day is your new day. Each day you're getting closer in finding the strength to persevere. We need to stop thinking that we are not successful in networking and looking over the fence to see that the grass is greener for others in our network. If you do see the grass being greener on the other side of the fence, please realize that their water bill is much higher to keep the grass so green!

To reach your goal, you need to learn to energize your network to gain support and draw upon the strengths of others in your network. Once you have learned to incorporate the factor of energizing your network to make things change, you will also realize that things have to change. Changes always present new challenges, and realization of these changes is never easy. There are some changes that we make ourselves and some changes are imposed on us, for example political turmoil, unemployment, additions to the family, or loss of a beloved one. The current difficult times we are faced with including financial, spiritual, emotional or physical may cause us to question our dreams, vision, goals, ambitions, enthusiasm, or ability to remain perseverant. Our belief that we must abandon our dreams or ambitions because the current times have become too hard regarding the circumstances we are facing or a situation that we never asked for or never experienced before, is something that we need to get control of. Because a look back in history, will show us that history is repeating itself, and others who have faced situations worse did persevere by staying focused and energizing their network to make change occur in their lives!

In networking, not every moment of every day will be a success story – you have to make it a success story by looking at what you have instead of what you don't have. That's why it's so important to have a vision of where you have to come from and where you want to go to, so that you can compare before, during, and after to sustain yourself during networking. Not everyone will agree with your vision, or the way you approach your goal, but remember, it's your personal goal.

From the first day your network was started, it grew based on your value system and how you treated others in your network. In your daily networking story there will be naysayers who want you to give in, give up, and not let you into their network. If they don't share your value system, then it's not a loss to say good bye to these people and move on. Networking means you NEVER give up! Follow your dreams and visions and reach them by accomplishing what you set out to do – stay to your own value system and your strengths will outweigh your weariness! You may have to rethink the process and make adjustments to your networking style or approach in today's society, but if what you want to accomplish and contribute in networking is important, it can withstand adjustments.

Let me tell you my networking story about bringing President Clinton the first time to the Netherlands... and please remember, it was not easy; it was almost a catastrophe and a failure in non-measurable fashion. So sit back and read how it turned out.

It all started on August 15th, 2002, when I sat in the office of the person who was trying to arrange President Clinton's visit to the Netherlands. He asked me if I would help him selling tables for the event President Clinton would be speaking at. I immediately questioned if he was truly bringing the 42nd President of the United States, President William Jefferson Clinton, to Holland. He was talking about the event being in two months and at that moment – it was August – he still did not have a confirmation that President Clinton was truly coming. Besides, I didn't hear anything about this from certain people in my network, like the US Embassy and the American Chamber of Commerce (AmCham) in the Netherlands. I knew they would have had to know that something like this was going to happen, because it would be one of the first times a former American President would be visiting the Netherlands. It was just over 6 months that President Clinton had left office, and I could not believe he would be visiting Holland that soon. However, the person who was trying to arrange it was convinced that President Clinton would be coming. He didn't have the official confirmation in writing. As this gave me the feeling that things were not as sure or locked in as he thought, I quickly shifted from selling tables to becoming a partner in the organization and with his permission I made a few calls from his office to confirm what he was saying. At that moment I was extremely inspired, motivated, and enthused for getting involved as a partner and helping make the event a success.

So I quickly thought: "Who do I know that knows the former President?" Of course, that was the US Ambassador to the Netherlands, the Honorable K.

Terry Dornbush, whom I knew to be a very approachable man. Throughout the years, Ambassador Dornbush had become a good friend of mine during his time in and out of office in the Netherlands, where he decided to reside, and my time in and out of the military. I called him in Atlanta, Georgia, where he happened to be at that moment.

"Sir, Ruf here. Ambassador, I need to arrange for former President Clinton to come to the Netherlands as the guest of honor at a business function hosted by a client of mine. How do I get through to his office, sir? Can you help me?" I said.

The wheels began turning and the necessary links formed in a matter of seconds. "If necessary, Ambassador," I continued, "We'll fly you to President Clinton's office to clinch the deal. This event has to go on."

"No, that's not necessary, Ruf," he assured me. He then advised me how to contact the appropriate person and also suggested that I let his successor, Ambassador Cynthia P. Schneider, know what I was trying to do, which of course, I did.

The former Ambassador Schneider was cycling in North Carolina when I connected to her, and I asked her if she could help me arrange to bring former President Clinton to the Netherlands. In turn, she confirmed the appropriate contact that Ambassador Dornbush had provided. Then, I immediately called the scheduling office for President Clinton and began arranging the visit.

The Scheduling Officer told me that President Clinton was not scheduled to visit the Netherlands in October 2002 and there were NO plans or intentions to do so. Wow, what a direct answer to my question and an eye opening experience to say the least! Then he instructed me to call President Clinton's booking agency. The booking agency told me that there wasn't any sort of so-called agreement the person said he had with them to bring President Clinton to the Netherlands. So it was not true and now the person who said he had arranged everything was the one who had "egg on his face" and turned to me asking if I could help him. What to do now? I looked at him and clearly told him President Clinton would not come and whoever was keeping him on the line was just pulling his leg and in fact was not telling him the truth. He immediately panicked, because he had been very busy arranging everything and now was putting his representation on the line to his network about bringing President Clinton to Holland in two months. Well, as a professional networker and a former soldier, I saw the opportunity to jump in and secure my position in the organization and my price tag for coming to his rescue and helping him. I knew he was in no position to negotiate and he needed my assistance. Besides, he also was in a very bad position with his network and had to save face. After setting my price tag, we agreed that I would start immediately making things happen in my network. For those who are wondering what my price tag was, well it was 10% of the price he would pay to bring President Clinton to the Netherlands, 50 event tickets (for individuals involved in my Giving Back Foundation), ten people in the VIP room to meet President Clinton (my family and best friend) and four people to sit at the Head Table with President Clinton (my Giving Back Ambassadors, me and of course Herma).

The first obstacle was already before me, and I had to remove it to move onto the next stage of networking – **securing President Clinton!**

So I contacted President Clinton's booking agent again to ensure them that I wanted to bring President Clinton to Holland under the umbrella of The Networking Corporation. I knew that it would be much easier for them to screen and do a background check on me, seeing that I was an American and a retired soldier. The networking wheels started rolling, and quickly I faxed a confirmation to President Clinton's scheduling office that we had the program worked out with their booking agent, and we had a green light to bring

President Clinton for the first time to the Netherlands. He would arrive not in October, but in December 2002. With a lot of perseverance and enthusiasm, I turned a potentially failed visit into a very successful networking experience! But now I had to move on to the next obstacle – **another speaking engagement**. They wanted President Clinton for another event in Holland two days later. Now I had to negotiate for two speaking engagements for President Clinton in a way that it would fit into his two days schedule, because he for sure would not stay in Holland for another night! After several days of decision making and maneuvering with President Clinton's office, we eventually worked out a schedule that President Clinton would arrive in the Netherlands on Friday to give his speech. He would then head to another engagement in Europe, only to return to the Netherlands for a second speech and then head back to the States. My second obstacle was gone now. We could start preparing everything, and I moved onto the next stage of networking – **preparing inspection!**

As we would host President Clinton on two separate dates and times for our events, we had to prepare two locations, one in a town called Zeewolde and the other one in Rotterdam. Due to this unique scheduling situation, the booking agency sent someone over at the end of September to coordinate the visits with the organization and me. The visit and inspection of the locations and facilities went very well, and they were impressed with our professionalism. So everything was in place for President Clinton's visit to the Netherlands on December 13th and December 15th of that year. We continued preparing to fill up the room with people that wanted to meet and network with President Clinton. In just a few weeks we had over 1,200 people who registered for our Friday event in Zeewolde and everything was running smoothly, up until ten days before December 13th. Without any notification or warning, we heard and read across different news and radio stations that the Mayor of Zeewolde canceled President Clinton's visit to his city because of the security around the event. The Mayor wasn't able to estimate the possible risks involved in such a large event, so he had to withdraw and inform the organizer that the event with President Clinton could not be held in his town of Zeewolde. Wow, what a surprised change of events! Everything was arranged and just ten days before the event would occur, we had to regroup and come up with a contingency plan, a backup plan – something I learned in the military. We quickly assembled everyone involved in the operation including security, catering, marketing, public relations, sales, administrations, sponsors, etc. Everyone and anyone who was involved were assembled.

Then I thought: Wait, we have President Clinton coming back two days later on the 15th in Rotterdam, so let's move the event to Rotterdam and find a location that could accommodate 1200 people and give a secure environment!" I called and informed President Clinton's team and together we worked out a press release. We needed to respond quickly and firmly that President Clinton was visiting the Netherlands and there was no doubt of that fact. This is what it stated:

Rotterdam, December 4th, 2002

The Honorable William Jefferson Clinton, 42nd President of The United States, is coming to the Netherlands on December 13th, 2002. . . that is now being held in Rotterdam, in place of Zeewolde, the Netherlands. The times of the afternoon and evening program remain the same but will be held in Rotterdam. We will see all our guests in Rotterdam on December 13th, 2002. For further information please contact...

Try to imagine you are planning a big event with everyone in your network attending, and out of the blue you hear that the location is not available. But my third obstacle was broken through, and I moved onto the next stage of networking – **the new location!**

Of course we had to rearrange everything now, but first we had to find a new suitable location for the event and one that would be approved by President Clinton's team. After all, they had just been screening and approving the former location in the Netherlands a few weeks before. Thank goodness we were able to quickly find one in Rotterdam that could accommodate our event on short notice.

Now we could fully concentrate on our preparations at the new location, so things were back to normal and on track. Up till the morning of the event... you will not believe what happened. And no, there was not an earth quake, the location did not burn down, and President Clinton was not sick. Something much worse happened while President Clinton was on his way to the airport. Secret Service informed him to turn around and go back home! President Clinton would NOT be getting on that plane and flying to the Netherlands on Friday, December 13th, 2002. Yes, I know, it was Friday the 13th. Are you possibly thinking why would someone plan something on that day? Well, that someone is not superstitions and does not believe in unlucky days. Yes it's me, and I don't believe in luck, only in faith. The faith before me now was the fact that President Clinton was not coming that day. I needed to act not out of the spirit of fear, but out of the spirit of power, of common sense, and the spirit of perseverance. I had to think how to make this work while trusting that everything would work out.

It was eight o'clock in the morning, and the constant ringing of my phone awakened me. I also had 23 missed calls. I had just arrived home about 4 hours before after doing the final checks at the location and walking the parameter with President Clinton's Advance team. They told me that it was all over the news and on the radio stations that President Clinton was not coming to the Netherlands for our event that would start in eight hours. I couldn't believe what I was hearing. What were we going to do? We had 1,200 people coming, the press, Herma, and my family! I started praying for guidance and was hoping I would be filled with the ability to find a solution to this awful unforeseen and almost unbelievable situation.

Holding firm to my faith and hoping that this event with President Clinton would truly go on as planned, I learned very quickly what perseverance and enthusiasm is all about, because you cannot and will not let your network down. I gave them my word, so my reputation to make things happen was on the line, the right things that reflect my true character and follow my value system.

Everyone was caught off guard again and we had to assemble the whole team to figure out how we would go on with the event and regroup things after taking this hit from the blind side. We just had to get up and dust ourselves off and get our ducks back in order. After arriving in Rotterdam at the Command Center, I instructed the organization to inform everyone that the event would be postponed till further notification, because we were sure that President Clinton would not be having dinner with us that night in Rotterdam with our 1,200 guests. I requested to be put into a room and not to be bothered until I worked out things with President Clinton's team on the ground in Rotterdam and in the United States. We came up with different scenarios on how we would be able to make this happen and not let our networks down. After hours of brainstorming, we decided that since he was already planning on coming back to the Netherlands for the second event – remember, we had him booked for Sunday December 15th, 2002 at 12:00 in Rotterdam – we could ask him if he would just close out his first speaking engagement and travel 10 minutes over to the second speaking engagement and then head back home. We thought it was a great plan, we all agreed that it could work, and it would be easy to inform all our guests, sponsors, press, and our team that President Clinton would be coming at the same time, same place, only on a different date. We were all enthused that faith, perseverance had overcome the situation, and things would work out just fine. There was still one more hiccup. President Clinton needed to agree too, but they couldn't ask him at that time because he was sleeping. We had to wait till around 4pm that day to get the green light from President Clinton that he would do two speaking engagements on December 15th, 2002. Arranging and rearranging everything to make this happen overcame my fourth obstacle, and I moved onto the next stage of networking – **the actual event!**

Over the past few months, I worked intensely with numerous agents and officers of the President, particularly his Advance Teams, who thoroughly checked out the venue where he was scheduled to speak. I had the honor and privilege of working closely with them, including spending some treasured downtime playing cards. Wish I had my "Ruffle Shuffle" NetworKing card game developed at that time, because then we could have played cards using my special networking cards!

Never in my wildest dreams did I ever think that I would be playing host to a former U.S. President and ultimately sitting with my family and close friends at the head table with him.

But sure enough due to my networking efforts, on December 15th, 2002, the honorable William Jefferson Clinton, 42nd President of the Unites States, came to The Netherlands.

You can bet that it was worth the hassle and the effort when the US former Commander in Chief shook my hand, and to my total surprise, said to the audience during his speech: *"I want to give a special thanks to my dear friend, Charles Ruffolo, who made it possible for me to come to Holland."*

Mission accomplished and success achieved. The client was happy, and I was thrilled to have been able to make it all happen. By energizing my broad network and building a rapport with the former President's office, it all came together. In the heat of battle, your network does not abandon you – and vice versa. If I say that something will happen, I do everything possible to make it happen. That's because I know how to energize my network. Obviously, you can do the same. After all, if a wayward boy from Pittsburgh can get through to a United States President, or anyone else for that matter, so can you!

On the runway at Rotterdam airport, President Clinton asked me if I would like to fly back to New York with him. Unfortunately, I had to turn him down because, believe it or not, I had other commitments to keep that involved quality time with my wife and family. "Maybe next time, Mr. President!"

From that first experience with President Clinton, I have had the honor to host him several times in the Netherlands, attend several Clinton's Global Initiative (CGI) events, and visit him at his home in Westchester, New York, when I successfully hooked him up with the Dutch Postcode Lottery. To this day, I still work with the Clinton's Foundation and the CGI. He even sent me several thank you letters! My fifth but not my final obstacle was breached, and I moved onto the next stage of networking – **getting paid!**

Not until after I had to take legal action against the organization that I worked my butt off to help, assist, and put my neck on the line, I finally was paid on August 15th, 2006! So after I started working with the organization back in August 2002 and the event was finalized on December 15th 2002, it took me four years before I got paid. That's right, it took 1460 days and nights before they paid me – and believe it or not, it was in five installments. This is a behavior that was totally against my value system of trust, respect, integrity, and empathy, but I did show them my enthusiasm to get my fair share and my perseverance eventually won.

Please understand that not everything works out as planned, and not everyone is going to play by the same rules and value system as you do. Sometimes you have to take extreme steps and actions to get your networking story correct. By the way, there's much more to this networking story, but I will keep that till my next book if you don't mind!

We are working every day to achieve our goals and don't give up a value system that is built on faith, hope, enthusiasm, and perseverance to make important achievements in your networking life. Celebrate every milestone of your networking journey to wherever it is you are trying to go.

Albert Einstein said: *"It's not that I'm so smart; it's just that I stay with the problem longer."*

Following illustration I read on the Internet relates to our daily networking life: A psychologist walked around a room while teaching stress management to an audience. As she raised a glass of water, everyone expected they would be asked the "half empty or half full" question. Instead, with a smile on her face, she inquired: "How heavy is this glass of water?" Answers called out ranged from 8 oz. to 20 oz.

She replied: *"The absolute weight doesn't matter. It depends on how long I hold it. If I hold it for a minute, it's not a problem. If I hold it for an hour, I will have an ache in my arm. If I hold it for a day, my arm will feel numb and paralyzed. In each case, the weight of the glass doesn't change, but the longer I hold it, the heavier it becomes."* She continued: *"The stresses and worries in life are like that glass of water. Think about them for a while and nothing happens. Think about them a bit longer and they begin to hurt. And if you think about them all day long, you will feel paralyzed – incapable of doing anything!"*

It's important to remember to let go of your stresses. As early in the evening as you can, put all your burdens down. Don't carry them through the evening and into the night. Remember to put the glass down!

ENTHUSIASM

Enthusiasm is an intense and eager feeling that moves or motivates you from within by the power of God.

I think one of the greatest stepping-stones I learned as a young boy was this: If you do something, do it with enthusiasm. From the streets of Pittsburgh throughout my military career into the business world, I saw that enthusiasm

91

is contagious.

We always have to be careful that we are not becoming obnoxious in our enthusiasm. That we show our enthusiasm not it in a way that puts somebody else down or turn people off in our network.

I would like to spend some time with you thinking about the stepping-stones of success in networking. I call these the value stones; values that you can put your feet solidly on, and values that help you get through life. They help you get through the storms, through the dark nights, and through the raging rivers of life. If you keep your feet on your value stones, you can cross life on dry land.

Make no mistake about it; enthusiasm can change your life and the lives of others in your network for the better. Enthusiasm energizes everyone. But remember, no one can make you enthusiastic, because enthusiasm doesn't come from the outside. I hope you get this point and clearly understand that honest, realistic, and healthy enthusiasm comes from within!

It's helpful to discover what enthusiasm is. Enthusiasm is not merely excitement. Excitement is an external substitute for genuine enthusiasm, and it's the result of stimulation from the outside. No doubt some of you can get excited about certain sporting events such as the Pittsburgh Steelers winning the Super Bowl for the sixth time or getting a new car. Excitement comes from outside and enthusiasm comes from within. You can remember that because the word "excitement" begins with "ex" meaning "*outside*," while the word "enthusiasm" begins with "en" meaning "*inside.*"

The word "enthusiasm" comes from two Greek words, "*en*" and "*theos*," and it means "to be moved or motivated by the power of God from within." Spiritually speaking, enthusiasm means that God is working in our lives giving us the desire and power we need to please Him. The world calls us to be excited – stimulated by external circumstances.

Enthusiasm is not zeal without knowledge. A zealous person without knowledge is nothing more than a fanatic. A fanatic is a person who has re-doubled his efforts after losing sight of the objective. Properly understood, enthusiasm is the fervor of both reason and revelation. We are not enthusiastic despite what we know; we are enthusiastic because of what we know.

Enthusiasm is not emotionalism or excitement, nor is it the energy of the flesh, rather enthusiasm is energy working within and through us for our good. Enthusiasm is the fuel of action and the surest precursor of success. Your enthusiasm can have a profound effect on others. When you approach anything with an upbeat commitment to get the job done, people begin to take notice. When they see that you believe in what you are doing, they become willing to join the process. The secret, then, is to pour your life into something that captures your heart and give it all you have got. You will find that your zeal is contagious, and it will be spread to the people around you. Enthusiasm can change our lives, it can influence everything we do, and it can affect all our relationships. Yet we cannot generate it by simply saying: "*I'm going to be more enthusiastic*"- that's the energy of the flesh. Others cannot generate it in us - that's excitement.

Let's energize our network together enthusiastically! Do others see the special enthusiasm in you that reflect the inner peace and joy you have? It's not just through the good and happy times that they watch us. It's also through the difficult and trying times that they look to see that we have something different about us. Something that carries us through those challenges and that encourages us to not give up. Enthusiasm is not about being a cheer leader and shouting for joy everywhere you go. Sometimes enthusiasm is just sticking to a cause and embracing a belief because you know it's truth and worth clinging to. In everything you do, no matter how dull or boring it may seem, greet each task you do with enthusiasm because it does matter.

Enthusiasm is not based on how fun your job is or how much it pays. It's based on why you do what you do. Make others see your enthusiasm reflected in your convictions, your perseverance, your good times, and your challenges. Make your enthusiasm be a contagious zeal that draws others to the things you are doing at work or in your life.

I use enthusiasm as we use honey to attract bees. I use enthusiasm to attract attention toward my network, toward doing business. Possessing enthusiasm catches people's attention in your network and causes them to sit up and take notice of what you're saying or doing. Your enthusiasm draws attention to who you are and what you stand for in your LIFE! Remember Chapter 1 (Character & Behavior) where I mentioned the particular values that form the blocks of our networking L.I.F.E: Love, Integrity, Faith, and Enthusiasm.

Nothing can stop a person who is filled with enthusiasm. He or she will keep going no matter what, because they know they are doing the right thing for the right cause and for the right reasons!

In this chapter, I talked about "Perseverance & Enthusiasm." These are two things that make you race to the finish line and never give up or feel under the gun. Like the lyrics in the song, "Born to be Wild," so clearly state: *"Racing in the wind, and the feeling that I'm under."* You are never out of the race!

"Enthusiasm is the yeast that makes your hopes shine to the stars. Enthusiasm is the sparkle in your eyes, the swing in your gait. The grip of your hand, the irresistible surge of will and energy to execute your ideas."
Henry Ford

CHAPTER 7

SUCCESS & FAILURE

"I've missed more than 9000 shots in my career. I've lost almost 300 games. 26 times, I've been trusted to take the game winning shot and missed. I've failed over and over and over again in my life. And that is why I succeed."
Michael Jordan

SUCCESS

Success is the accomplishment of an aim or purpose.

OK, I want you to do something. Please raise your hand if you want to be successful in what you are doing or want to do. No matter if you are reading this book at home, in the train or bus, or at work, just raise your hand. And if someone thinks you want to say something, just say: "I am going to be successful," and if you are at home just ask: "Can I get an Amen". . . Haha-ha!

Now raise your hand if you want to fail at what you are doing or want to do. Did you raise your hand? I hope not, because who in the world sets out to do something and wants to fail from the beginning? I think we all want to be successful at what we are doing, and from the get go, we all want to reach our goal or obtain the successful results. But often life is not that easy; we will be faced with obstacles and walls that hold us back or make us think that we are not going to succeed, but going to fail. Let me tell you about some of my successes and failures, so you can see and read that I too am not always successful. And if you don't believe me, ask Herma because besides the blessings of success, she also has bearded the scares of failure. Remember, some things in life fall apart so that better things can fall together. And no matter how many mistakes you make, or how slow you progress, you are still way ahead of everyone who isn't trying!

There are people who say you must belong to this club, that organization, you only are important if you do everything right, have enough money, have enough education, or have all your ducks in order. Well let me tell you: that's wrong!
Perhaps for most of us, not knowing what is coming next is the most terrifying of prospects. In networking, we don't know our actions or where our actions will take us; we only have faith and hope that our actions will lead us to success in our lives. If we know what's coming, we are able to prepare ourselves mentally, physically, emotionally, financially, and spiritually. But if we don't know what's coming, we are thrown into uncertainty, stress, chaos, and possibly failure. The only ability to reach success is to dive into the depth of wisdom, faith, hope, and continue applying the values and norms of networking.

In life and in business, always calculate success and failure because you cannot always win, be number one, get the job, get the partner you dream of, or keep all your hair. Yes my hair is falling out, but I did once have a lot of hair. And I still have a lot of hair on the back and sides of my head!

Often we see everyone around us succeeding, and in the social media we see everyone being happy. It even looks like some are having the time of their lives... it seems like everyone is so successful and doing so well. I hope you are successful, but I also hope that you make your success what you want it to be, not what the outside world, the media, and the people in your network want or think your success should be. Success is what you determine yourself and not what others in your network determine for you. Protect yourself and accept the down side if you are not as successful as you hoped. You probably are wondering right now what I mean with the downside.

Let me give you an example of what I mean with success and failure. When hosting Sir Richard Branson for several days in the Netherlands, someone asked him: "What are some of the fundamental rules for running a business and being a successful business person?" Richard answered with this: *"There is a fundamental rule for running or being a business person and that is protecting the down side. When we started our airlines, Virgin Atlantic, I already had a successful record company. I knew starting an airline was risky, so I rang up a Boeing company and said that I wanted to buy a second hand 747. But I didn't know if the airlines would work or not, so I wanted to be able to hand back the plane after 12 months if it did not work. This way, it would not bring the whole Virgin Group down. They agreed, so I protected the down side. The banks, however, did not prepare the down side. They went from a lending spread to where they did not know what their down side was, and it has been mind blogging, because I know some of these people running these banks and they just got completely out of control. So they literally put the world in parallel as a result. Generally speaking, I don't think any of them should be in business at all. So governments had to rescue the banks by stepping in to make sure that they saved the banks. Effectively if they did not rescue the banks, all the hundreds of millions of personal decent companies would have gone bankruptcy for no fault of their own. I think the governments at large have done a good job stepping in and rescuing the banks."*

In business and in life, we must calculate the risks of success and failure in combination with the downside and the consequences of our actions and behavior. Being successful will take time; when we look back on our entire life, we will see that success is often ahead of us and may not come over night. Once we start something and put it into our network or the market, we don't know how the market will react to our services, products, our actions, or our behavior. But I'm sure we all set out to be successful and to eliminate the risk of failure.

But how do you measure success and what are your success stories in your life? Did you earn the position on the sports team, did you win runner-up in the contest, did you cook your first meal, did you save as much as you hoped for, did you complete the report, or did you inspire others in your network? Did whatever you accomplish make you feel good? Are you happy with reaching something and satisfied with your accomplishments today? Then look in the mirror, because you are successful!

Sir Richard Branson stated: *"Success and money can contribute to happiness, but happiness itself is another thing altogether. Words like 'family', 'friends', 'love' and 'laughter' have a lot more to do with happiness than words like 'gross', 'capital' and 'revenue'."*

Build into your heart, mind, and soul that success is what you determine and no one else. Be competent and learn the skills of networking, gain knowledge from others, and increase your ability to do good things and good work. In The Networking Academy, a program that I started and improved together with Anne Marie Westra, who is the Co-Founder, we use this phrase to emphasize what participates will gain from following The Networking Academy's Course. They will "enhance their skills, develop their capabilities and find their way to success." The key to success is finding what success means to you – try it; what do successes mean to you and when was the last time you achieved success?

OK, do you want to know what I think is my most successful story or legacy in networking? Actually you should know, because if you know something about "the Rufman," you know I'm all about giving back to others. I always talk about it and emphasize during my training, workshops, and lectures that the cardinal rule of networking is giving (I will tell you more about that in Chapter 9, "Giving Back & Love*"). To get in life, you have to first give. So to me, starting my Giving Back Foundation is one of my most successful accomplishments in my life.

GIVING BACK FOUNDATION (1999)

In my book, "*Network Your Way To Success*," I have written extensively about my Giving Back Foundation, where there are no rules or regulations, but values: Hope, Respect, Responsibility, Enthusiasm, and Generosity. Still today, I am extremely proud of this non-profit foundation that gives high achieving and motivated youth in the Dutch society, the opportunity to improve their academic performance, set career goals, learn job skills, and develop high working standards in order to grow up as successful citizens and eventually business people. It is rather extraordinary that Giving Back does not receive any government funding and only functions from private donations from companies and people who want to give back to society, which I am very grateful for.

Since 1999, the Giving Back Foundation has helped young people from all over the world. These individuals have learned through their experience with Giving Back that they are able to meet and work with people from extremely diverse backgrounds. While these young people are brought up in very diverse home environments, our goal is not to change them but to help and guide them.

To date, the Giving Back Foundation is operating in more than 24 high schools in all the major cities in the Netherlands. Hundreds of youth from 15 countries have gone through our Giving Back program, thanks to our many sponsors and mentors from all walks of the business community. Giving Back is essentially "networking to help others." We give back the same benefits that we reap.

THE GIVING BACK STUDENTS COMMUNITY (2010)

Students who have properly completed the Giving Back program and study at universities or colleges may become members of the Giving Back Students Community (GBSC), a club that is run by Giving Back students. The GBSC organizes many activities, study tours, and (sporting) events designed for the students during their studies. This way they are able to complete all their knowledge and skills and to give insights to build a successful career in business or government after their graduation. The GBSC finances these activities through membership fees, a contribution from students, and financial support from the Giving Back Foundation.

Being a member of the GBSC also offers students the opportunity to be coached by a professional during their studies. This coach is employed by one of the partners/main sponsors of Giving Back.

THE GIVING BACK PROFESSIONALS (2013)

In 2013, former students of Giving Back started the "Giving Back Professionals," an organization that maintains Giving Back participants that have ever been involved in Giving Back over the years – and there are thousands of them – together to focus on keeping the spirit of Giving Back alive.

There are so many examples of success stories within the Giving Back community, but the one that stands out the most to me after more than 13 years is that a former student, Aylin Cengioglu – who works as a registered accountant with customs in Amsterdam and is 30 years old – is a mentor herself now and gives back to someone else who is or was in a similar situation as she. That is what Giving Back is all about, keeping the spirit alive – Thanks!

More information can be found at www.givingback.nl and www. gbsc.nl.

FAILURE

Failure is lack of success, an unsuccessful person, enterprise or thing.

While success is achieving the maximum of your potential in the situation you are in, failure is not a matter of not reaching your goal! Failure is failing to give your project or activities all that you have, demanding too much of yourself, setting the bar too high for yourself, not knowing your limitations, and/or just not being physically or mentally capable to take on the task at hand.

There are not that many things more awful than the feeling of failure. Failure directly attacks our ego, our image, our inner self, and our sense of who we are in relation to our network. Failure brings with it fear, anger, shame, and anxiety. When we fail, we feel impotent, inadequate, depressed, dazed, destroyed, isolated, and betrayed. The pillars of our life are shaken, the mountain to our success is crumbly, and the ground we walk on is sinking. Failure is the "F" word (NO, I'm not talking about the other "F" word) that we don't want to hear or talk about in our network. We try to stay clear of someone infected by it because it may be contagious.

There are many books, articles, and movies about success, but not too many people write about failure or in fact talk about their failures. This made me decide to address the "F" word and tell you about some of my personal failures and what they brought me, my relationship with Herma, my family, and my network. I know what it is to be in need and not to have, but on the other side of the coin, I know what it is to have a lot and plenty of something. Through the school of hard knocks, I have learned that the secret of being content in any and every situation or circumstance, whether success or failure, well fed or hungry, living in plenty or in need, being part of a network or not, is that you have to stop thinking about what you don't have. You need to think about what you do have and be very grateful that you have faith, hope, and love!

Every time we dare to start new things, like changing a job, starting or expanding a business, beginning a relationship, moving to a new country or town, we all risk failure. Every time we reach out, we will be off balance and poised to fall. But we have to keep reaching out to get our success in life. We must never forget to listen to our gut feelings and to the ones that love us.

Handling failure is difficult and most entrepreneurs, as I am too, are born optimists. I refuse to think about the possibility of failure. I believe in myself, and I believe that success is just around the corner or that the deal is in the pipeline. What reinforces this view in me is that, whenever something is likely going to fail, I very often get hired to give another workshop, training, lecture, or obtain a new paying member for my Network Club. I get encouraging feedback from my network, which only keeps me going and gets me more enthusiastic to continue networking.

Failure can be experienced in many ways. A business can fail, you can lose your job, fail at school, have a broken relationship, underperform at work, get passed over for a promotion, or fail in love. We are faced with failure daily, but it's just how you deal with the situation.
How much failure in their networking life a person can take, all depends on the individual and his or her determination to succeed. Realize that failure is an integral part of the growth in your networking life. To expect and think that your life and the process of networking are always smooth sailing is to invite a lack of realism into your life. You will recover from failing, and the bonus of failure is that you will get opportunities to improve yourself, gain knowledge, insight, experience, and wisdom.

Failure is a given in life, so please understand that every person on earth has good times and bad times; each of us will have successes and failures in their lives. We will have obstacles, setbacks, and outright failures, but the most important aspect of failure is what we learn from it. In the face of adversity, rejection, and failures, you must continue believing in yourself and refuse to consider yourself a failure. I have learned more from my failures than from my successes. My failures allowed and helped me rise to the next level of understanding myself and deal with life in general. Failure provided me with the time needed to reflect and learn how I can climb the ladder of success.

You cannot run away from failure or hide from it, but you can learn to resolve failure and confront it straight on. If others were able to face failures, then why can't you? Failure is a test that keeps reappearing in our lives. When we pass these tests, we become stronger each time we face them. Failure actually makes us sturdy and less fragile. To be able to realize that our labor is not vain, we must be steadfast and immovable. Failure turns us into wiser networkers. It helps us not only to learn from our own mistakes, but also from the mistakes of others. Learning from mistakes of others can save us time, energy, and resources that we can put into other productive uses. When we honestly have attempted our ultimate best, then we have been successful in the spite of failure. What we need to do is to not only tell others in our network success stories, but more importantly our stories of failure, so we all can learn from it. Here is a short story of the awful and scary moments of failure that have brought my network and me through triumphs and tragedies, pains suffered, and lessons learned.

Sit back and listen to this networking story that at the time was not successful. It is about times when I lost six figures, that's right you read that correctly, I lost six figures on something that after a few months I already knew was not going well. I got this feeling inside that this project was just not good. You know the feeling when your mind, heart, and soul are saying that things just don't sound right. I was blocking out these feelings, because I was seeing that pot of gold at the end of the rainbow. Man do I wish I had listened to my gut feeling and also to the voices of the people dear to me, who kept telling me that this project just didn't add up.

It all started by someone reading "the Aircraft carrier story" in my book, "*Network Your Way To Success*." How within 36 hours, I arranged an aircraft carrier for two multinational Dutch companies who wanted to do a sale promotion off the coast of Barcelona, Spain. This person had this very challenging project and wanted me to get many more large steel flowing vessels. The project seemed solid and, as all the i's were dotted and the t's were crossed, I jumped into this project.

At the time, I had a very trustworthy network (and I still do!), and I always could deliver on what I said I would. So I energized my network and got several very high profiled people from my network involved in this project. We invested money, time, energy, and our networks. As a matter of fact, I got my family to invest too and even had my nephew fly over several times from the States to the Netherlands to be involved. We believed that we were all being honest and truthful to each other. However, that was not the case. After two years, the project was dead in the water. All the time, money, and effort put into the project didn't deliver the results we hoped for. We lost a lot of money and energy from something that could have been avoided if I would have read the writing on the wall. You know that expression?

"The writing on the wall," or "the handwriting on the wall," is an idiom for "imminent doom or misfortune" and for "the future is predetermined". It originates from the Book of Daniel (Old Testament), Chapter 5, from the handwriting on the wall that was witnessed at a banquet hosted by King Belshazzar. As those at the feast profaned the sacred vessels pillaged from the Jerusalem Temple, a disembodied hand appeared and wrote on the palace wall the words, "Mene, Mene, Tekel, Upharsin". The prophet Daniel was summoned and interpreted this message as the imminent end for the Babylonian kingdom. That night, Belshazzar was killed and the Persians sacked the capital city.

Concerning my situation, I, The NetworKing, should have read "the writing on the wall" given the signals that Herma and others saw and understood! My painful experiences and failures motivated me to share with you the insight I gained from it. If I look back on the failures in my life, I can honestly say that they not only taught me that failure is a part of networking and no one is spared from it, but also made me a better person!

I always remember listening to my very good friend, Stedman Graham, during his lectures and workshops reading from Dee Groberg's book, "The Race: Life's Greatest Lesson." It's an illustrated poem and heart-wrenching story of a boy in a footrace, hoping to win, but falling again and again. By reading it, I hope you will get just as much inspired as I did.

THE RACE POEM

"QUIT! GIVE UP! YOU'RE BEATEN!" They shout and plead,
There's just too much against you now, this time you can't succeed.
And as I start to hang my head in front of failure's face,
My downward fall is broken by the memory of a race.

And hope refills my weakened will as I recall that scene.
For just the thought of that short race rejuvenates my being.
A children's race, young boys, young men; now I remember well.
Excitement, sure, but also fear; it wasn't hard to tell.

They all lined up so full of hope. Each thought to win that race.
Or tie for first, or if not that, at least take second place.
And fathers watched from off the side, each cheering for his son.
And each boy hoped to show his dad that he would be the one.

The whistle blew and off they went, young hearts and hopes of fire.
To win, to be the hero there, was each young boy's desire.

And one boy in particular, his dad was in the crowd,
Was running near the lead and thought, "My dad will be so proud."

But as he speeded down the field across a shallow dip,
The little boy who thought to win, lost his step and slipped.
TTrying hard to catch himself, his hands flew out to brace,
And mid the laughter of the crowd, he fell flat on his face.

So down he fell and with him hope. He couldn't win it now.
Embarrassed, sad, he only wished to disappear somehow
BBut as he fell, his dad stood up and showed his anxious face,
Which to the boy so clearly said,"Get up and win that race!"

He quickly rose, no damage done - behind a bit, that's all,
And ran with all his mind and might to make up for his fall.
SSo anxious to restore himself to catch up and to win,
His mind went faster than his legs. He slipped and fell again.

He wished that he had quit before with only one disgrace.
I'm hopeless as a runner now, I shouldn't try to race.
But, in the laughing crowd he searched and found his father's face
That steady look that said again, "Get up and win the race."

So, he jumped up to try again. Ten yards behind the last.
If I'm to gain those yards, he thought, I've got to run real fast.
Exceeding everything he had, he regained eight or ten,
But trying so hard to catch the lead, he slipped and fell again.

Defeat! He lay there silently, a tear dropped from his eye.
There's no sense running anymore - three strikes and I'm out - why try?
The will to rise had disappeared, all hope had flown away.
So far behind, so error prone, closer all the way.

I've lost, so what's the use, he thought, I'll live with my disgrace.
But then he thought about his dad, who soon he'd have to face.
"Get up," an echo sounded low. "Get up and take your place.
You were not meant for failure here, get up and win the race."

With borrowed will, "Get up," it said, "You haven't lost at all,
For winning is not more than this, to rise each time you fall."
So up he rose to win once more. And with a new commit,
He resolved that win or lose, at least he wouldn't quit.

So far behind the others now, the most he'd ever been.
Still he gave it all he had and ran as though to win.
Three times he'd fallen stumbling, three times he'd rose again.
Too far behind to hope to win, he still ran to the end.

They cheered the winning runner as he crossed first place.
Head high and proud and happy; no falling, no disgrace.
But when the fallen youngster crossed the line, last place,
The crowd gave him the greater cheer for finishing the race.

And even though he came in last, with head bowed low, unproud;
You would have thought he'd won the race, to listen to the crowd.
And to his Dad he sadly said, "I didn't do so well."
"To me you won," his father said, "You rose each time you fell."

And when things seemed dark and hard and difficult to face,
The memory of that little boy - helps me in my race.
For all of life is like that race, with ups and down and all,
And all you have to do to win - is rise each time you fall.
"Quit!" "GIVE UP, YOU'RE BEATEN." They still shout in my face.
But another voice within me says, "GET UP AND WIN THE RACE!"
Dee Groberg

Stedman's lifelong partner Oprah Winfrey said at the Harvard 2013 Commencement Graduation: *"Learn from every mistake because every experience, encounter, and particularly your mistakes are there to teach you and force you into being more who you are."*

Failure can be made to feel like the worst thing that could ever happen to a person. With failure comes frustration, bleak and gloomy feelings, and creating a situation when we think there is no need to continue the work we started or to pursue our dream. Failure takes the wind out of your sail, the air out of your balloon, and blinds you from the unlimited opportunities that are right in front of you. Failure happens to the best of us.

Remember, behind every success story are tales and networking stories of failures. A success story is never complete without passing through tales of failure. Failure makes victory taste sweeter.

When failure challenges us to think and triggers new ideas to make our ultimate goal attainable, it turns into opportunity. If we are willing to shift our focus into this perspective, our network will be able to extend a helping hand. Those in our network will smile at us and will be happy with the work we are doing. Then failure is actually a blessing.

Never let a bad day make you feel like you have a bad life. Just because today is painful doesn't mean tomorrow won't be better. If you don't like something, change it. If you can't change it, change the way you think about it. Your mistakes and failures should be your inspiration, motivation, and enthusiasm, not your excuse. Just think of a team that loses and is motivated to win the next game, and the boxer that loses the fight who is motivated to regain the title. The only failure that can truly hurt you is choosing to do nothing, because you are too scared to fail again. Failure is not falling down; failure is staying down when you have the choice to get up again. You should never let one dark cloud cover the entire sky. The sun is always shining on some part of your life – if you have ever flown in an airplane you know that as the plane rises above the clouds in the sky, the sun is always shining up there. Sometimes you just have to forget how you feel, remember what you deserve, and keep pushing forward above the clouds.

Your mindset is at the heart of your success. Just take the good with the bad, smile with the sad, love what you have, be thankful and blessed for what you have, and not for what you want. No matter how chaotic your past has been, your future is a clean, fresh, wide-open slate. What you do with it is up to you!

Read about some very successful people, who once failed in their lives, yet never regarded themselves as failures.

Wolfgang Amadeus Mozart, a musical composition genius, was told by Emperor Ferdinand that his opera, *The Marriage of Figaro,* was "far too noisy" and contained "far too many notes." Wolfgang Amadeus Mozart was dyslexic.

Vincent Van Gogh only sold one painting in his lifetime! He sold just one to a friend. Despite that, he kept painting and finished over 800 pieces. Now everyone wants to buy his paintings. His most expensive painting is valued at $142.7 million.

Albert Einstein didn't speak till he was four and didn't read till the age of seven. His parents and teachers thought he was mentally disabled. He only turned out to be a Nobel Prize Winner and be the face of modern physics. A Munich schoolmaster told Albert Einstein, the greatest thinker of our time, that he would "never amount to much." Albert Einstein was dyslexic.

Richard Branson, billionaire mogul of Virgin, has had his share of failures. Remember Virgin Cola or Virgin credit cards? Probably not. He has lost hundreds of millions of dollars, but has not let failure stop him. If you want to, you can rent his private island for $ 53,000 a night. Richard Branson has dyslexia.

Walt Disney was the man who gave us Mickey Mouse and Disney World. His first animation company went bankrupt. A news editor fired him because he lacked imagination. Legend has it he was turned down 302 times before he got financing for creating Disney World.

Steven Spielberg applied and was denied two times to the prestigious University of Southern California film school. Instead, he went to Cal State University in Long Beach after which he directly went on to direct one of the biggest blockbusters in history. In 1994, he got an honorary degree from the film school that rejected him twice. He now is worth $ 2.7 billion. Steven Spielberg has dyslexia.

Stephen King's first book, *Carrie,* was rejected 30 times and he threw it in the trash. His wife retrieved it out of the trash and encouraged him to resubmit it. Today, Stephen King has sold more than 350 million copies of his books.

Many record labels rejected **The Beatles**. In a famous rejection, the label said: *"Guitar groups are on the way out"* and *"The Beatles have no future in show business."* After that, the Beatles signed with EMI, brought Beatle mania to the United States, and became the greatest band in history.

Michael Jordan is famous for being cut from his high school basketball team. He turned out to be the world's greatest basketball player and never let failure deter him.

Thomas Edison, the most prolific inventor in history, was considered unreachable as a youngster. No list of success from failures would be complete without the man who gave us many inventions, including the light bulb. He knew failure wouldn't stop him. *"If I find 10,000 ways something won't work, I haven't failed. I am not discouraged, because every wrong attempt discarded is another step forward."* Thomas Edison was dyslexic.

Joanne "Jo" Rowling was unemployed, divorced, and raising a daughter on social security while writing the first Harry Potter novel. The rest is history.

Oprah Winfrey was fired from her television-reporting job because they told her she was not fit to be on screen. Oprah turned out to be one of the most successful and wealthy women in the world.

And now about myself. I was given a high school diploma to get me out of school and forced to join the military. I earned my Master's degree and successfully created The NetworKing Corporation, The NetworKing Academy, and the Giving Back Foundation. My mistakes and failures are my inspiration, motivation, and enthusiasm. I wrote bestsellers in English and in Dutch. I'm dyslexic.

The world attributes much importance to wealth, power, and status. But what if your wealth, power and status were gone, what would you have left? You would have your heart and that matters in networking because that will endure forever to others in your network!

Albert Hirschman, an American economist stated: *"The only way in which we can bring our creative resources fully into play is by misjudging the nature of the task, by presenting it to ourselves as more routine, simple, undemanding of genuine creativity than it will turn out to be."*

I couldn't express it better. As an entrepreneur, I often plunge into new projects and concepts, because I operate under the delusion that what I am attempting or getting involved in is not that risky and will work. But then, halfway down the road, I discover the truth, something others realized much faster than I did.

In our success and failure journey, we have a tendency of looking back to the good old days, hinking about the things we missed, all the opportunities we didn't take, and think about how things are not the way they should be in our success and failure journey. We reminisce and recall our past experiences or events: "If I would have been in that relationship, things would be much different than today." or "If I would not have entered the military and stayed in Pittsburgh, my life would have been a bunch of roses with the perfect job" – please! On the flip side of the coin we dwell on the future, the unknown, and think about how someday this or that will happen. You know, that "someday I will be standing on the greenest grass in the neighborhood" – again, please! Stop living in the past or the future, just focus on today and be satisfied with what you have. As it is said: do not worry or be anxious about tomorrow, for tomorrow will worry or be anxious about itself.

In this chapter, I placed the attention on the true meanings of success and failure, knowing that as children, we always want to succeed and be born again away from our failures. Sing it out as the song goes: *"Like a true nature child, We were born, Born to be wild."*

"Life is pretty simple: You do some stuff. Most fails. Some works. You do more of what works. If it works big, others quickly copy it. Then you do something else. The trick is the doing something else."
Leonardo da Vinci

112

CHAPTER 8

NETWORKING IN THE MODERN WORLD

"I'm the most recognized and loved man that ever lived cuz there weren't no satellites when Jesus and Moses were around, so people far away in the villages didn't know about them."
Muhammad Ali

While writing this book, I not only wanted the front cover of my book to stand out in a special way. I also wanted to do something different with the back cover. So my business partner, Anne Marie Westra, suggested using a QR (Quick Response) code, which turned out to be a terrific idea – Thanks Anne Marie. As you can see on the back cover, the QR code uses a square pixilated barcode that links directly to my special website. I used modern technology to simplify and conveniently link my printed book to digital content for your guide to inspiration, motivation and enthusiasm!

For those who don't already know, Denso Wave, a Toyota parts manufacturer in Japan, invented the QR code in 1994 to track production in his factories. Today, the QR code still is a relatively new tool for authors and book designers, and I decided to use it as a creative manner to get people to visit my website or to follow me on my social media platforms.

Using a personalized QR code offers me a highly interactive and personal experience to communicate with my network. Scanning the QR code gives you the power to decide if you want to engage and network with me directly which could turn out to be stimulating and rewarding for you. For example, you find related material about networking and my book, or you may be able to join a competition to win related products. By using networking applications, you will get the chance to be more successful.

Now onto how you can use modern technology to effectively network. How can you market yourself and stay in the mind of others in your network? Like the saying goes: *"Out of sight, is out of mind,"* if you don't see someone frequently you will forget about this person and he or she will fade out of your mind. When situations change, friendships may change as well. If the bonds are strong, it doesn't necessarily mean the end of the friendship. If you created your network on the principle of a strong value and norm system, your network will follow you your entire networking life. I hope you understand that words have the power to create and destroy things and should not be thrown around without thinking about the consequences. While networking on the World Wide Web or on the different social media platforms, make sure you choose your words carefully.

As I said before, in networking, you always have to hold on to your values and norms, especially when using social media platforms. You have the ability to protect your character and behavior in the global market by the information you give out. With the growing usage of modern technology, one may think that everything placed on the Internet or social media platforms is actually true. But stories may have been twisted, altered, distorted, or not from a first-hand source. Someone may even play with the feelings or emotions of others within their network. Be careful not to be the blind leading the blind, as the saying: *"Know the truth, and the truth will set you free."* If you have doubts, just do some investigating. Due to the power of modern technology, you will be able to quickly find out if someone is telling the truth or not. Modern technology allows us to share our life experiences with people around the globe in the blink of an eye. You hear about social media just about everywhere you go – there's no escape from it! And, believe it or not, it's not just only for kids anymore; almost everyone is using or talking on social media. Social media has become a dominant force in our lives, work place, and on the Internet it's no longer just used for casual purposes. But understand that if you pull out the plug, cut off the power, or your server crashes, there's nothing left of it. So it's very important that you can always rely on your most powerful form of communication: "Real life" networking or networking "in person," which was there from the very beginning and will always be there to the end. Technology is there in order to maintain an excellent relationship with our network.

Relationships are the essence of life. Every contact is all about either giving or receiving something. When you help someone, it's all about giving (as will be discussed in Chapter 9). Giving can be as simple as a smile, a good report, a referral, or a helping hand. Anything that encourages, inspires, contributes to someone else's well being, or adds value to him or her improves our happiness and is referred to as receiving. Social media works in the same way; you are giving information to others and you are receiving information from others.

OK, the best way to define social media is to break it down. Social media is instruments, technology, software, hardware to communicate, newspapers, or radio. So social media is the social instrument for communication in our society and networks today.

What is social media? Social media is a form of electronic communication through which we, the users, create online communities or generated content to share. We share our information, ideas, personal messages, pictures, videos, and so on of our community-based environment to interact, share, and collaborate with others in our network. Social media itself is an encompassing term for sites that provide radically different social actions. Twitter for example is a social site designed to let people share short messages or updates with others in their networks. Facebook, therefore, is a full-blown social networking site that allows for sharing updates, pictures, videos, joining events, and a variety of other activities.

Social media consists of many online tools and websites that encourage people to interact with companies, brands, and other people – even celebrities and journalists. Social media is a two-way communication stream, whereas with traditional media, messaging is published through a one-way communication stream to the masses, e.g. radio, television and newspaper.

Social media is about conversations, community, connecting with personalities, and building relationships within our network. It's not just a broadcast channel or sales and marketing tool for companies; it is our authenticity, honesty, and open dialogue to others following us or wanting to be in our network. Social media not only allows you to hear what others are saying about you, but also enables you to respond to their comments or remarks. As I mentioned before, think before reacting: be swift to hear and understand the message and slow to speak or respond to things on social media platforms. How many times have you had to "eat" your words because you spoke too quickly? Your supple responds will turn away wrath, but a harsh word will stir up anger and you even could end up receiving a warning message. If only we could see the full effect of the words we use, we would think twice before saying or writing those words!

Be compelling, useful, relevant, and engaging in using social media platforms. Be aware; always keep in mind that what you place on the Internet will never go away, not even by deleting it. It may stay veiled from our eyes, but never from the eyes in the sky! The Internet is like a big billboard. It might help you for every time you want to post something on a social media platform, you ask yourself, if it would be ok if it were shown on a billboard. If not, then just don't post it. Always stay true to yourself, no matter what.

But do not be afraid to try new things. You can benefit a great deal from using social media platforms to improve your communication skills, your human resources, and to enlarge your sales and marketing benefits. Today, customers can communicate and deal with your image, brand, and company through social media platforms.

We have all heard the age old saying: *"The customer is King,"* but the evolution of all the social media platforms has taken this adage to a completely new level. Today, the social end user is truly the King who has more power than ever before. You see, by using social media we can change the balance of power completely. We now are able to be very proactive by accessing the latest content from any company, brand, or individual at any time of the day from anywhere in the world, and it's fairly anonymous. Navigating to that brand's Twitter feed or Facebook page and engaging as we are followers and friends, shifts the balance of power. We can virtually raise our hands – by liking, following, commenting, sharing, or otherwise interacting. Only problem is that the company or brand doesn't know much about us at all.

For us as the end users, it's just incredibly empowering and therefore creates a set of expectations of how we think social media should work for us. This set includes expectations of control by allowing us to choose how and when we consume social content, expectations of accessibility by giving us access to an individual's or company's information, and expectations of speed by providing us with the latest information.

But this exchange not only can shift the balance of power in favor of us end users, but also of the company or brand. They control the frequency and intensity of the relationship; pushing out content they choose whenever they want. Only at that point, users can react by engaging, ignoring, or unsubscribing altogether.

Social media doesn't just change the means through which we engage with our network, potential clients, or unknowns. It changes the very balance of power inherent in the relationship with others in our network, and makes us moving targets on the World Wide Web. For as established we think social media is now, it will continue to evolve particularly in the recognition of the psychological and sociological factors that drive our behavior.

Social media use is a hard habit to shake. You try to stay away, but your fingers are itching for one quick click and another good scroll to last you through the day.

This may seem a little overwhelming at first, but don't be discouraged. The best way todip your toes into social media is by joining a community that best suits you or sounds the most interesting to you. Follow others in your network to see how they are managing their social media platforms, listen to social conversations, and ask friends or colleagues who are already users of a service for their insights. This will help you better gauge if social media is right for your goals, and gives you some ideas on how you could use social media to meet those goals.

Like everything, it's better to moderate social media. Use it wisely to start and nurture relationships in your network. Don't let it replace personal interactions or foster bad behavior, because at the end of a day, when a power outing cuts off all electronic means of communication, we still have our human brain that is faster than any computer in the world! Computers could be as smart as the human mind, but when you start talking, it's just pure intelligence. We are able to recall, remember, show emotions, and I think therefore we humans are many, many years ahead. Humans can integrate information from many different variables and stimuli. We can learn from experiences, observations, and experimentation. Computers can't easily adapt to changing situations. Moreover, the things that make us truly unique are that we have emotion, empathy, self-awareness, ambition, hope, faith, and love; things that are far beyond the capacity of computers!

Yes, I am using the various social media platforms too. As a matter of fact, Anne Marie Westra (there she is again) controls them all and she is very good at it. She successfully taught and showed me how I can market and promote myself, and add my business activities to my network in the best possible way while staying true to my values and norms. Now I have even accounts on Weibo (Chinese hybrid of Twitter and Facebook) and YouKu (Chi nese You Tube)! And what about you? Are we already connected in the social world? If not, let's get connected today!

In this chapter, I addressed networking in the modern world. Social Media is consuming lots of time out of our lives. But get used to it, because it will never stop. It will only increase, as the next and last couplet of the song: *"We can climbed so high, I never wanna die."* Now onto Chapter 9, the final chapter: "Giving Back & Love." Enjoy!

"I think it's fair to say that personal computers have become the most empowering tool we've ever created. They're tools of communication, they're tools of creativity, and they can be shaped by their user."
Bill Gates

CHAPTER 9

GIVING BACK & LOVE

"We make a living by what we get; we make a life by what we give."
Winston Churchill

GIVING BACK

Giving back is freely transferring the possession of (something) to (someone); handing over.

From a very early age, I have learned that my life is inspired and driven by the need for me to give back to others in my network. Even if I don't have it myself, I have the need to help others by giving them what they need. This may sound a little crazy, but I just don't feel good inside or happy if I cannot do something for someone else.

If you have read my book, *"Network Your Way to Success,"* you already knew that I grew up in a close-knit family. My family showed me that we had every type of profession and occupation right there at our very core, and I only needed to tap into my familial network for whatever it was that I needed. So I learned very quickly that you have to give to receive, and if you didn't give something to othern your network, you would not receive anything back. Life is like that, and please don't be fooled to think that it's not.

Most likely, your family is somewhat similar. Surely your network is more wide and varied than you think. I can guarantee you that every single person with whom you get in contact with has some connection to your life! Throughout each and every day, there are countless opportunities to connect you to people, places, and things that can benefit your life, and in turn, benefit others. Will you choose to ignore those opportunities or will you choose to listen to *"Your Wake Up Call"* and give to others in your network?

Because of the many reasons that giving is important – not only for the other person, but also for yourself – it's a critical element you need to develop in your networking life. I will first talk about why I think giving, "my daily medicine," is such an important concept. Second, I will give you some simple examples of how I include different aspects of giving in my daily life that allows me to hear my own *"Wake-Up Call."*

Giving is essential to our physical health – and I'm not talking about going to the gym or running on the track – and our spiritual, mental, emotional, and social well-being. Giving increases our self-esteem and enlarges our personal empowerment, because giving stimulates the release of endorphins, which has been linked to improving the function of our nervous and immune system. Endorphins are natural pain killing substances found in our brain that are produced during excitement, pain, consumption of spicy food, and love .They make us feel well, comfortable, happy, and relaxed. So truly giving is our medicine to a healthier life! Some of the things we gain by making giving a greater part of our lives are a sense of empowerment, pride, happiness, security, peace, love, and feeling of accomplishment.

As I said, I have to give because I need to help others. It makes me feel good about myself, because I do something for someone who at that moment is not able to do it for him/herself. It enriches my life by developing new skills and growing as a person. It also enlarges my social connections and makes me see life in a whole new light. I'm able to experience and see how others are worse off than me, yet still hanging in there with hope and faith in tomorrow.

Giving to others helps me take my mind off of my own problems and enables me to see the bigger picture in life. Once I see the difference I can make in the life of others, my own confrontations in life seem smaller and much more manageable. Giving to others helps me to grow and explore interesting and challenging opportunities that might never have come along otherwise. Yes, giving allows me to experience a sense of increased value and greater self-worth which boosts my self-esteem.

When you give with joy, selflessness, and love, you will benefit greatly. The attitude you bring to giving will reflect the benefits you gain. Our world could be a much different and better place if we all would give something of ourselves to others. When you give to others or give your time to meaningful causes, things change. No matter what your life circumstances are, we have the ability to give. When we think about it, we know countless people who have made a difference in our lives by giving; positive as well as negative. So why not make a decision to have a positive impact on the lives of others by giving?

One of the most important reasons that I need to give back is to know that I am needed. Being forgotten is an awful feeling, so for me feeling needed and appreciated are critical in my life. Maybe we don't get that appreciation from our job or home life, where the things you do are expected or taken for granted. Giving makes you realize just how much you are truly needed.

Here are a few simple ways to give back to others in your network. I use these methods daily to help myself while helping others.

The smile. Did you smile today? Do you remember when you gave that smile to someone at your office, on the train, at school, or when you saw your friend or loved one? Giving someone a smile enriches our lives very much. I would recommend adding lots of smiles in your daily networking. Smiling is a very natural response that shares our happiness and joy with others in our network. Smiling triggers activity in our brain and that is something that I need a lot of... active brain cells. When we give a smile, there is a serious mind-body connection to our left frontal cortex to our brain, the portion of our brain that registers happiness. It pumps all kinds of feel-good endorphins into our brain – remember those endorphins I talked about earlier in this chapter. So smile today, no, smile at the next person you see, even if it's not your mother, father, brother, sister, friend, or an attractive person across from you on the bus or train – just smile. If you give others a smile, you will see that you are really making a difference in someone's life. And that's a great feeling!

The hand. Another way of giving I have built into my daily routine is giving someone a hand. A handshake, a hand in helping them up, a high five, a hand in getting them the job, a hand in staying focused on their dreams, or a hand in inspiring and motivating them to reach their success. Learn to give others a hand and you will receive a handful in return. Just reach out to others in your network and give them a hand.

Sometimes we are scared to ask others for a hand with things, because they may think differently about us or look down upon us. You may think asking for a helping hand shows you are weak or not capable to do it by yourself – so what? In networking, you have to use all means given to you to reach your success. Often, people have too much pride to ask for assistance or help, when indeed they need a helping hand. So reach out your hand to others in your network and support them as you would want them to support you. And every time you do so, you are further in building your network on a solid foundation of giving and love.

We build our lives taking one step at a time, and we realize that we will need a helping hand from others in our network. We think we can do it by ourselves and then we get *our "Wake- Up Call,"* a shock that makes us realize that our hands are full and we need someone else's hand to help.

Giving enriches our lives with meaning, fulfillment, and happiness. It allows us to unleash our full potential and create breakthroughs in our networks. In fact, it's a privilege to give. So give your time, knowledge, wisdom, wealth, and love and experience the power and beauty of giving!

My most successful relationships were built with people that I do more for than they do for me. I just give and give, without ever wanting or asking something in return. "But why and how can you live or work like that?" you probably want to ask. Actually, it's very easy. If you never give me something back, then I learned something about who you really are. A person that lives and works on the motto: *"Me, Myself and I"* doesn't go too far in life.

Often, people in my network send me a message or call me with something like this: *"Hi Ruf, I'm working on a very exciting new project."* or *"I have something that I am sure your network needs or could use, can you introduce me to someone in your network so I can pitch it for support or funding?"*

Now they are talking about me energizing my network to approach Clinton, Branson, Oprah, Carlos Slim, Beyonce, etc...They really expect me to reply: "Sure, let me fire-off an email, sms them, or just call them immediately to make an introduction and setup an appointment."

Let's get serious people! It doesn't work that way. The reason people like Clinton and Branson are in my network and give me their time of day is because they trust me and know that I respect their time. Thinking that they are just waiting for your amazing idea or project is not realistic. These people have seen, heard, or been involved in all kinds of similar projects. Be-

125

sides, they don't need to make any more money or do something else for the good of society. Please wake up and smell the coffee!

Giving is a beautiful experience. People often think that they are not able to give because they have not yet achieved a certain level of self-actualization. Well let me tell you about Abraham Maslow's famous hierarchy of needs. Maslow was a psychologist who studied human motivation; leading him to create a pyramid showing what people need to be fulfilled with.

The base of Maslow's pyramid starts with our core physiological needs: air, water, food, shelter, warmth, sleep, sexual intimacy, and so on. The second level comprises our security needs: protection from the elements, social order, law, and so on. The third level includes our social needs: love, family, relationships, work, group, and so on. The fourth level consists of our ego needs: achievement, reputation, responsibility, independence, prestige, status, and so on.

Maslow originally placed self-actualization needs as the fifth level at the top of his model. These needs were satisfied through personal growth, self-fulfillment, and the resolution of personal potential. Later models placed self-actualization as a seventh stage, above two new levels: cognitive needs – knowledge, meaning, and self-awareness – and aesthetic needs – beauty, balance, and form. Others have added an eighth and final level: our spiritual needs, achieved through transcendence and helping others to achieve self-actualization. Maslow believed that needs must be satisfied in the order of the levels he described. He felt that only after a level had been reached, an individual could begin to work on meeting the next level of needs.

Striving to develop Maslow's self-actualization characteristics will bring much joy into your life. These characteristics will bestow on you more wisdom, stronger relationships, greater compassion, and internal peace. If you achieve self-actualization, you will be able to see situations with more objectivity and clarity. You will see problems as challenges and as growth opportunities. You won't rely on cultures and the environment to form your opinions. You will be able to protect your inner values. You will believe in justice. You will be able to embrace and enjoy all races, cultures, faiths, and differences. You will be accepting, understanding, and compassionate. You will be able to laugh at yourself and the human condition, and you will seek experiences that are deep, meaningful, and lasting.

It is believed that as we become more generous and thoughtful givers, we will also develop some, or all of these gifts. Whether you donate money or time, giving back is beneficial and not just for others in our network, but for yourself. The old adage: "*It's better to give than to receive*" is true after all!

LOVE

Love is an intense feeling of deep affection.

Love is the answer to the most fundamental questions of human existence. Without love, nothing else really makes sense or matters. The most fundamental characteristic of love is that it seeks the good of the others in your network. Showing and giving love is the main ingredient to success in life and business.

Love is completely accepting others as they are in your network. It's about being patient and kind. It stops us from being arrogant or rude, it doesn't cause us to be irritable or resentful, and it doesn't make us unhappy at wrongdoings. Love is the truth, love bears all things, love believes all things, love hopes all things, and love endures all things.

Love starts with you. You must like yourself in a way of taking good care of yourself physically, emotionally, spiritually, mentally, and socially.

If you like yourself, you will be able to like others in your network and they will like you back. If you don't like yourself, you will waste energy trying to please others in your networks who don't like you, or you will end up being in someone's network you really don't like.

One way to like yourself is to realize that you are not perfect. But that there are not too many others that can do the things you do just like you. The way you see the world is not quite the same way as others see it, and the talents, ambitions, or lack thereof that you possess is much different than others. No one screws things up the same way you do, and no one makes the same mistakes as you make. Just be yourself, and love yourself with all your faults and weaknesses. Remember, you are the way you are and people in your network will only love you for that!

Each of us has a unique value and belief system; a way of seeing the world that is slightly different to everyone else's perception. It's called your DNA, the hereditary material in you. It's what turns you on, what turns you off, what makes you special, and it determines why you are different. What we feel is important; our political preferences, tastes in food and music, and so on, all arise out of this value and belief system. Our particular thoughts and feelings resonate with different aspects of the world around us.

Take me, for instance. I like Italian food, because I was raised on that type of food and it makes me feel good to think back on my youth. I'm able to think back to my mother, Clara Elizabeth Welch-Ruffolo, who died at the very young age of 50 when I was 15 years old, and whom I loved very much. But the values and norms system she gave and instilled in me lives on. She instilled in me a value system that grew from faith to hope, trust to respect, integrity to empathy, perseverance to enthusiasm, success to failure, and giving back to love. This is a value system that still today influences my character, attitude, and behavior toward my own self and others in my network. From the foundation of the value system our parents taught us, common thread in this book, we will come into harmony or conflict with other types of people that come into our lives and will be affected by our values and belief system. We all make choices: where to live, which sports team to join, which supermarket to shop at, what organization to be a member of, or what network to be associated with. All these choices reflect our values, beliefs, and our way of being. Our personality is reflected in the places we turn up at, and so we end up being surrounded by people who are the same way, have the same values and norms as we do, and make the same choices.

Sometimes, when my financial investment into a new concept or project is not giving me the return, it causes me to feel like I made another big mistake. Deep down, I think that this is the time to beat myself up, and I feel like I am not good enough. During those times, I definitely need my *"Wake-Up Call,"* the call to turn the negative energy into positive energy and get my butt out of this situation. I need to pick myself up from the ground, not feel sorry for myself, and kick it into high gear to take back control of the situation. I don't have a spirit of fear, but a spirit of power, a spirit of love, and a spirit of a sound mind.

Because the consequences of not taking any action will have an effect on my physical and mental health, I turn to my faith and talk with my wife to get back on track. Additionally, in my mind I talk to myself in a way I would talk to someone else in my network that would be in the same situation. I need to talk to myself this way, because I'm the one who put me in this situation and I will be the only one who can change it. If you ever end up in a bad situation, remember that others in your network will be there for you to give you a helping hand, but you really have to do the work yourself. Sometimes when other people put you down, try to make you feel bad, or hurt you, remember the words: "*Sticks and stones may break my bones, but words will never hurt me*" – and walk away with love still in your heart!

Let me end this book with a story about love in its most true form. It's a story of an unconditional love that was shown and given to me when I was 18 years old and it changed my life forever. I told you, being the youngest of the family; I was a wayward young man growing up in Pittsburgh. When I reached the age of 18, all my brothers and sisters where gone, living in other cities and I was the only one left in the house. At that time I didn't know that my brothers and sisters had been talking with each other about whether I would be taken in and live with one of them, or they would put me in the military. Well my brother, Bobby or "Olo," came back from Vietnam where he had served the U.S. Military, and he told me that I had to get out off the streets of Pittsburgh quickly and join the military. I always looked up to him and often listened to him – I said often, not always.

One day, he picked me up and drove me to the Federal Building in downtown Pittsburgh to talk with a Military Recruiter to see what my options would be. Bobby wanted me to join under the Vietnam Era, so I could get all the benefits, like the G.I. Bill, college tuition, medical insurance, and other great things. By the way G.I. means, Government Issue that you would receive if you joined the military. So he asked me which service I wanted to join: Marine, Air Force, Coast Guard, or Army. "Army," I said because he was in the Army and so was our father, who served in the US Army during the Second World War in the Phillipines, and our grandfather, who served in the Italy Army during the First World War.

The Recruiter told me that if I was serious about joining the military, like my brother said, I would have to take the Armed Services Vocational Aptitude Battery (ASVAB) test. This test would determine how qualified I was for certain military occupational specialties and possibly enlistment bonuses. Then my brother told me to sit down and take the test right there. When I asked him why, he said: "Because then we immediately can see what your options are when you enlist in the military." So I sat down in a private room and took the test. Guess what? What score do you think I received? Despite trying my very best, I failed the test. Bobby was surprised that I didn't pass the simple military entry exam. He looked at me and said: "How could you fail this test?" He wondered what I had learned in school, and now he knew that I was worse off than he thought. He looked at the Recruiter and said: "He will be back with me in hand, so get the paperwork prepared because he is going into the military."

Not too far from the Recruiter's office, Bobby stopped by a library and he signed out several books on how to prepare for the ASVAB test and some other books he thought I would need to read. We got back into his car and drove off toward his house. Once we arrived at his house, he started preparing things in a room. He put all the books on a table, looked at me and said: "I love you, Bone, so you will stay in this room for a week to study and prepare yourself to retake this military test. I'm locking you in this room and you can only come out to go to the bathroom." I looked at him and said, "What?" And he said: "You heard me, so get your butt into that room and get started .You need to concentrate on learning and preparing yourself for the test, because this is about your future that you need to get the most out, brother!" So I stayed locked in that room for a week – of course I was fed and let out to go to the bathroom – but I studied, slept, ate ,and got frustrated in that room. After the week was over, Bobby let me out, I got cleaned up, and we drove back to the Recruiter's Office. I sat down and took the test again, but this time passed the entry exam for the military, with a very high score – YES, this was a success, based on true love!

I looked at the Recruiter and asked him what my options were, because now he could determine how qualified I was for certain military occupational specialties and an enlistment bonus. He said that several occupations were available to me, but there was one that sounded more interesting than the other ones. This was working with Special Weapons. I asked him what that occupation consisted of and he said he didn't know because it was all secret. I told him I wanted to take that job, and after the Recruiter gave his permission, we signed a Delay Entry contract. This meant that I was officially in the military. I would ship out two days later after passing the military physical test, which I did with flying colors!

After the formal part of the enlistment, I asked Bobby why he wanted me to do this so quickly and without even informing or telling my friends on the corner. He said that if I would have told my friends, they either would have talked me out of it or they would have wanted to go with me. This idea was not good for me, the military, and certainly not to our country. So I had two days before shipping out, and I was very eager to get back to the corner to inform all my friends and of course the ladies that I joined the military. On the other side of the coin, Bobby had to inform the family that it worked out, and I was leaving Pittsburgh and the street corners.

When I look back on the twenty years I had been in the military and almost twenty years in the business world now, I am abundantly blessed to have so much love in my life. Joining the U.S. military and being stationed in the Netherlands, gave me the love of my life, Herma, whom I have known for more than 35 years. We have been married for 33 years –YES, we are very grateful.

I can't wait to walk new trails in my life, because it will get me into situations that continuously develop my character and behavior, bringing great joy and strength to my faith, hope, and love for myself and others in my network.

The words of this closing chapter, "giving back" and "love," enrich my life and give me a feeling of freedom, living in a state of nature, and networking with an immeasurable level of intensity like the final words of the song clearly express, *"Born to be wild, Born to be wild!"* To keep inspired, motivated, and enthused in your daily life, please always remember that eventually:

Failure will turn into Perseverance – Perseverance will turn into your Character – Your Character will turn into Hope – Your Hope will turn into Trust – Your Trust will turn into Empathy – Your Empathy will turn into Love – Your Love will turn into the values you hold dear in your heart and soul.

"No one is born hating another person because of the color of his skin, or his background, or his religion. People must learn to hate, and if they can learn to hate, they can be taught to love, for love comes more naturally to the human heart than its opposite."
Nelson Mandela

CHAPTER HIGHLIGHTS - QUOTES

For each chapter title of this book – "*Your Wake-Up Call*" – I chose two powerful words that truly enable me to be and remain inspired, motivated and enthused in my day-to-day life. To reinforce my message, each chapter itself starts and ends with a quote from someone I am truly inspired by or whom I personally know.

I hope while reading them, you will become just inspired as I did while choosing them. Maybe one of these quotes will even sum up the entire message for you or relates to you personally!

CHAPTER 1: VALUES & NORMS
"Your beliefs become your thoughts, Your thoughts become your words, Your words become your actions, Your actions become your habits, Your habits become your values, Your values become your destiny."
Mahatma Gandhi

"If we aren't willing to pay a price for our values, if we aren't willing to make some sacrifices in order to realize them, then we should ask ourselves whether we truly believe in them at all."
Barack Obama

CHAPTER 2: CHARACTER & BEHAVIOR
"A good character is the best tombstone. Those who loved you and were helped by you will remember you when forget-me-nots have withered. Carve your name on hearts, not on marble."
Charles H. Spurgeon

"All you have in life is your reputation: you may be very rich, but if you lose your good name, then you'll never be happy. The thought will always lurk at the back of your mind that people don't trust you. I had never really focused on what a good name meant before, but that night in prison made me understand."
Sir Richard Branson

CHAPTER 3: FAITH & HOPE
"You will not enter paradise until you have faith. And you will not complete your faith until you love one another."
Prophet Muhammad

"And so I tell you, keep on asking, and you will receive what you ask for. Keep on seeking, and you will find. Keep on knocking, and the door will be opened to you. For everyone who asks, receives. Everyone who seeks, finds. And to everyone who knocks, the door will be opened."
Jesus Christ (Luke 11:9-10)

CHAPTER 4: TRUST & RESPECT
"I know God won't give me anything I can't handle. I just wish he didn't trust me so much."
Mother Teresa

"If a man is respectful he will not be treated with insolence. If he is tolerant he will win the multitude. If he is trustworthy in his word his fellow man will entrust him with responsibility. If he is quick he will achieve results. If he is generous he will be good enough to be put in a position over his fellow men."
Confucius

CHAPTER 5: INTEGRITY & EMPATHY

"If a man is called to be a street-sweeper, he should sweep streets even as a Michaelangelo painted, or Beethoven composed music, or Shakespeare wrote poetry. He should sweep streets so well that all the hosts of heaven and earth will pause to say, "Here lived a great streetsweeper who did his job well."

Martin Luther King Jr.

"Leadership is about empathy. It is about having the ability to relate to and connect with people for the purpose of inspiring and empowering their lives."

Oprah Winfrey

CHAPTER 6: PERSEVERANCE & ENTHUSIASM

"If you live long enough, you'll make mistakes. But if you learn from them, you'll be a better person. It's how you handle adversity, not how it affects you. The main thing is never quit, never quit, never quit."

William J. Clinton

"Enthusiasm is the yeast that makes your hopes shine to the stars. Enthusiasm is the sparkle in your eyes, the swing in your gait. The grip of your hand, the irresistible surge of will and energy to execute your ideas."

Henry Ford

CHAPTER 7: SUCCESS & FAILURE

"I've missed more than 9000 shots in my career. I've lost almost 300 games. 26 times, I've been trusted to take the game winning shot and missed. I've failed over and over and over again in my life. And that is why I succeed."

Michael Jordan

"Life is pretty simple: You do some stuff. Most fails. Some works. You do more of what works. If it works big, others quickly copy it. Then you do something else. The trick is the doing something else."
Leonardo da Vinci

CHAPTER 8: NETWORKING IN THE MODERN WORLD
"I'm the most recognized and loved man that ever lived cuz there weren't no satellites when Jesus and Moses were around, so people far away in the villages didn't know about them."
Muhammad Ali

"I think it's fair to say that personal computers have become the most empowering tool we've ever created. They're tools of communication, they're tools of creativity, and they can be shaped by their user."
Bill Gates

CHAPTER 9: GIVING BACK & LOVE
"We make a living by what we get, we make a life by what we give."
Sir Winston Churchill

"No one is born hating another person because of the color of his skin, or his background, or his religion. People must learn to hate, and if they can learn to hate, they can be taught to love, for love comes more naturally to the human heart than its opposite."
Nelson Mandela

CONCLUSION

"Your *Wake-Up Call*" is the story of my life. In eight chapters, I have illustrated the most important aspects of my journey and the many challenges I had to overcome. But most of all, I offer you a glimpse into my daily life, one that was full of adventure with many ups and downs. How I overcame the sorrows of the worst of times, in order to experience the best times of my life. The plans I laid out for myself and what I had hoped to become had failed.

Throughout my book I tried to "Wake-You Up," giving you proof that by remaining strong through the hard times, your life WILL get better. "*Your Wake-Up Call*" is a combination of characteristics I believe a person must possess, in order to give them the ability to be inspired, motivated and enthused in everyday life. It is a collection of my moral principles, combined with a practical illustration of my actual experiences. It begins with the reminder that we must remain ethical at all times, holding our values and norms close to the heart, knowing exactly what they are, and the type of life they help us lead . After all, our values are not only the principles of right and wrong, or good and bad, but they guide us in our journey to build a "network" of life.

This book is your personal guide toward inspiration, motivation and enthusiasm. It's an inside look into the mind of an individual who is not only educated, but also a street-smart businessman that has had to deal with various situations concerning family, friends and business. I know what it takes to be successful no matter what the situation calls for; proper etiquette, social relationships, and the ultimate need for self-control within society or among members of a specific profession or network.

Please remember that each day will bring about new burdens, new doubts and worry-some nights, but tomorrow WILL offer a new spark of hope and the will to start over again. Our faith gives us the strength to endure and win the battle we call Life.

My wife Herma perfectly summarized THIS BOOK by saying:

Norms, values, live life by truth.

Have strong character, behave with love.

Don't ever give up hope... and faith will set you free.

It's here, in all of us.

I want to trust and respect you, I hope you will do the same with me.

Dare to feel what the other person is feeling – go there, with empathy and integrity.

Persevere, GO, Smile, be enthused with life... remember... it flies

Deal with failure... that alone is success!

Look around, don't just VIEW people as names, look them in the eye.

Modern-day networking in this world... doesn't have to be impersonal.

Love is the strongest emotion... feel it! And when you give love, it will be given back to you.

SOURCES

Books

Clinton, Bill, _My Life_ (Autobiography), (2004), Published by Knopf Publishing Group. Groberg Dee and Anderson Mac, _The Race: Life's Greatest Lesson_ (2004), Published by Simple Truths.

Maslow, A.H., _A Theory of Human Motivation,_ (1943), Originally Published in Psychological Review, 50, 370-396.

Oubelkas, Joseph, _400 brieven van mijn moeder_, (2009), Published by Literoza.

Ruffolo, Charles D.A., _Network Your Way To Success,_ (2011), Published by The NetworKing BV.

Websites

BrainyQuote®, (2001 – 2014), www.brainyquote.com

Merriam Webster Online Dictionary and Thesaurus, ©2014 Merriam-Webster, Incorporated, www.merriam-webster.com

Bible Gaterway, (2014), www.biblegateway.com

Wikipedia, (2014), www.en.wikipedia.org/wiki/Pittsburgh#Regional_identity

Video recording
Branson, Richard, (2010), ©Broadcast Organizers, the Netherlands.

Clinton, William J. (2004), ©Broadcast Organizers, the Netherlands.

Graham, Stedman, (2009), ©Broadcast Organizers, the Netherlands.

Music
"Born to Be Wild," Steppenwolf, written by Mars Bonfire,
Producer, Gabriel Mekler (1968).

Contact information
Charles D.A. Ruffolo - MPA
Professional Networker | International Speaker
Trainer | Moderator | Author | Publisher

Founder & Owner:

The NetworKing BV & RIBS Network
www.TheNetworKing.com

The NetworKing Academy
www.TheNetworKingAcademy.com

Giving Back Foundation
www.givingback.nl

The NetworKing B.V.
Kallenkote 31a
8345 HC Kallenkote
The Netherlands
Email: Ruf@TheNetworKing.com
Telephone: +31 (0)521 510 139
Mobile : +31 (0)6 502 87 672
Fax: +31 (0)521 510 179

Contact information
Charles D.A. Ruffolo - MPA
Professional Networker | International Speaker
Trainer | Moderator | Author | Publisher

LinkedIn:
www.linkedin.com/in/thenetworking
Twitter:
www.twitter.com/TheNetworKing1
Facebook:
www.facebook.com/TheNetworKing
Google+:
www.plus.google.com/CharlesRuffoloTheNetworKing

A very special thanks to Anne Marie Westra-Nijhuis
(EPLÚ Management Support – www.e-plu.nl)
for her remarkable dedication and commitment to The NetworKing
Thank you!

www.ingramcontent.com/pod-product-compliance
Lightning Source LLC
Chambersburg PA
CBHW062005200326
41519CB00017B/4679